PHILOSOPHY IN CULTURAL THEORY

What is the place of philosophy in cultural theory today? What might come of a confrontation between philosophy and cultural studies?

Despite its interest in theory, cultural studies in both Britain and the USA distanced itself from philosophy during the 1970s and 1980s. However, in the past decade this hostility has begun to give way under pressure from the globalization of cultural forms and the consequent need to draw on philosophical resources to deal with questions about universality and difference, totalization and abstraction. *Philosophy in Cultural Theory* offers a philosophical critique of cultural theory today.

Peter Osborne makes critical interventions into the central philosophical debates motivating contemporary cultural analyses: interdisciplinarity and the status of pragmatism; the relationship between sign and image; the technological basis of cultural form; the theoretical importance of translation; the temporality and politics of modernism; the conceptuality of art; and the place of fantasy in human affairs. Drawing on the legacy of Walter Benjamin and the *Communist Manifesto*, he establishes a new transdisciplinary perspective on the experience of modernity as cultural-historical form.

Philosophy in Cultural Theory will appeal to all students of philosophy, cultural studies and art theory, and to readers interested in the shifting role of interdisciplinary studies.

Peter Osborne is Professor of Modern European Philosophy at Middlesex University, London. He is an editor of the journal *Radical Philosophy* and author of *The Politics of Time* (1995).

PHILOSOPHY IN CULTURAL THEORY

Peter Osborne

London and New York

First published 2000
by Routledge
11 New Fetter Lane, London EC4P 4EE

Simultaneously published in the USA and Canada
by Routledge
29 West 35th Street, New York, NY 10001

Routledge is an imprint of the Taylor & Francis Group

Typeset in Sabon by
Florence Production Ltd, Stoodleigh, Devon
Printed and bound in Great Britain by
TJ International Ltd, Padstow, Cornwall

British Library Cataloguing in Publication Data
A catalogue record for this book is available from the British Library

Library of Congress Cataloging in Publication Data
Osborne, Peter, 1958–
Philosophy in cultural theory / Peter Osborne.
p. cm.
Includes bibliographical references and index.
1. Culture–Philosophy. I. Title.
HM641.O73 2000
306'.01–dc21   00-055315

ISBN 0-415-23801-3 (hbk)
ISBN 0-415-23802-1 (pbk)

CONTENTS

PREFACE

What might come from a confrontation between philosophy and cultural studies? The question has an air of theatricality about it, of a stage-managed meeting between the estranged parties of a lingering dispute, unsure if they are still enemies or might, one day, become friends.

Academic work is increasingly subject to the administration of disciplinary boundaries. Ironically, given its almost geological history in the West, for periods of which it was more or less synonymous with culture itself, philosophy has benefited from this reprise of disciplinarity. It has spent the best part of its recent institutional life honing the arguments for its existence as an autonomous discipline and for a privileged but rarefied place in the hierarchy of knowledges. Whether this hardening of boundaries has been such a good thing for intellectual life more generally, and its ability to foster theoretical comprehension of the historical present, in particular, is less clear. In the division of academic labour, philosophy for the most part occupies the barren heights of an absolute yet formal universality (frequently, nowadays, of a computational kind), while the new discipline of cultural studies gobbles up the present as lived experience, with a relentless drive to contemporaneity.

In so far as philosophical thought informs the new discipline, it is largely through rogue elements of the modern European or 'continental' tradition; displaced fragments, patched together in creative *bricolages* to suit the needs of the moment. In so far as the present impinges on the mainstream of the disciplinary practice of philosophy, on the other hand, it does so mainly through the technological trope of 'applied' ideas (ethicists as experts), at considerable remove from the textured structures of meaning and contradictory ideological forces that are the staples of cultural analysis. The revival of liberal political philosophy, through its engagement with issues of nationalism and multiculturalism, and the marginalized presence of a feminist critique of the philosophical tradition, are the exceptions that draw attention to the rule. However infuriating they might find the epistemological polemic of a renegade like Rorty, philosophers turned out from the mould of the 'cognitive science' side of the post-analytical tradition can hardly complain about the breadth of his influence, when they are themselves so patently ill-equipped to address the concerns of the humanities and social sciences. Yet philosophy has both its origins and its enduring non-denominational appeal in the idea of self-knowledge – a history of which the Italian Marxist Antonio Gramsci, grandfather to cultural studies in Britain, was keenly aware.

My previous book, *The Politics of Time*, was lucky enough to be reviewed in the *Times Higher Education Supplement* in Britain, twice: once in a section devoted to books in cultural studies, and again in one on philosophy. In the first instance, despite considerable sympathy for its project (an immanent critique of the philosophies of time and history innervating theories of modernity), it was judged, unfortunately, to remain 'within the limits of philosophy'. Later, subject to the gaze of a fellow philosopher, it appeared as a species of 'cultural commentary'.[1] It was consoling at the time to consider this antinomic rejection a dialectical success. On reflection, however, it became clear that a more direct approach to the mutual antagonism between the two fields was required. The essays that make up this book are the first fruit of such an approach. Each has its origins in a particular occasion – a lecture, a paper, notes for a panel discussion – but all have been revised, reworked or substantially expanded for publication here. Together they represent a linked series of interventions from a particular philosophical perspective (and perspective on philosophy) into some of the central debates in cultural theory – or at least, cultural theory in cultural studies. A word of warning, though, about the apparent homogeneities of the two fields.

Despite the relative unity of each field, constituted by their mutual antagonism, the problematics between which the book seeks to stage a confrontation are neither simple wholes nor can they be considered as empirically given: neither 'philosophy' nor 'cultural theory' can be confident of its self-identity. Their unities must be constructed – historically and differentially – rather than received. Second, their genealogies are closely related. In the European tradition, philosophy and cultural theory are as often to be found inside one another – philosophy in cultural theory, cultural theory in philosophy – as they are without. After all, for a certain German tradition, philosophy simply *is* the ideal reflexive form of modern culture as a whole. From this point of view, in its most essential determination, philosophy already is (or should be) cultural critique. Yet this philosophical ideal remains just that, an ideal, outside of an engagement with the totality of cultural objects and practices in the present – an engagement that philosophers have singly failed to undertake, restricting themselves in the main to an Arnoldian conception of culture as 'the best that has been thought and said in the world . . . the study of perfection'. This necessarily excludes vast bodies of significant practice and experience within Western capitalist societies and, given the ethnocentric formation of judgements of the 'best', has, historically, excluded whole non-Western cultures too.

Finally, and perhaps most importantly, philosophy must itself be understood, at one level, as a cultural form. Just as reflection upon its own formation has long been one of cultural studies' favourite tropes, so the formation – or at least, the reproduction – of philosophy as a disciplinary practice also falls within the domain of cultural analysis. This is by no means a merely sociological issue. Rather, it affects the meaning and legitimate range of application of philosophical concepts themselves. The more one inquires into the philosophical meaning of concepts in cultural theory, the more the cultural-historical status of philosophical concepts themselves appears as a correspondingly critical and equally neglected issue. This is never more so than in the extension of the problematics of Western theory to non-Western contexts, a transformative process which reacts back on our understanding of these problematics in their application to the West, and forms the avant-garde of critical self-consciousness in cultural theory today.

The essays in this book practise a philosophical critique of cultural theory as reflective judgement: reflecting upon concepts in cultural theory from the standpoint of their philosophical significance, extending their meanings beyond their original contexts; reflecting back upon the procedures and protocols of philosophy from the standpoint of such concepts, transforming the self-understanding of philosophical concepts in turn.[2] Such a practice is at once systematic in orientation and particular in content, seeking universality within the claims of particulars, building up a transdisciplinary problematic via a shifting constellation of terms.

Certain themes predominate: the forms of universality characteristic of general concepts in cultural theory; the relationship of pragmatism to metaphysics; technology and cultural form; the temporality and politics of modernism; conceptuality and *aesthesis*; the constitutive role of fantasy in human life – topics I take to be at the philosophical heart of cultural theory today. A particular author – Walter Benjamin – sets the theoretical course, with his concern for the conjointly historical, metaphysical and political experience of cultural form. But the aim is to practise philosophy as critical reflection, rather than to expound an established position independently of its engagement with current problems and competing perspectives.

Chapter One establishes the programmatic perspective on the fundamental affinity between a certain post-Hegelian philosophical tradition and the project of cultural studies from within which subsequent chapters explore particular problems or topics. The central issue in this chapter turns upon the anti- or post-philosophical thrust of the pragmatism of contemporary cultural theory, and the possibilities of an alternative, metaphysical pragmatist tradition, stemming from C.S. Peirce and the later

Nietzsche, which finds its main cultural-theoretical representatives in Walter Benjamin and Gilles Deleuze. The concern with a metaphysical pragmatism continues in Chapter Two in a critique of the Saussurean semiotics which provides the mainstream of cultural studies with its theory of meaning. This critique is pursued, first, via a reconsideration of Peirce's trichotomy of types of sign (icon, index, symbol) and, second, through an extended discussion of the historical ontology of the photograph, in which attention to technologies of imaging leads to a reformulation of the relationship between indexicality and iconicity. This reformulation is further elaborated via Peirce's theory of interpretants, in which his semiotics is integrated into his pragmatism via a naturalist pragmatics. The unmediated naturalism of Peirce's concept of habit is contrasted with the historical mediation, in Benjamin's work, between habit and the technological dimension of cultural form. The chapter concludes with a consideration of Deleuze's alternative appropriation of Peirce.

Chapter Three picks up on the issue of the form of universality characteristic of general concepts in cultural theory (with which the first chapter concludes) and explores it, first, via a translational model of theoretical generality, and second, with reference to the global generalization of the concept of modernism. Modernism, it is argued, is best conceived as a quasi-transcendental practical historical schema of universal but highly abstract significance. Its more concrete meanings and particular forms must be defined conjuncturally – independently of hegemonic historical models – by virtue of their temporal-political dynamics alone. Chapter Four returns to the *Ur-text* of modernism as a political form, Marx's and Engels' *Communist Manifesto*, and re-examines it from the standpoint of its literary, cultural-historical form. Taking issue with the one-dimensional modernism of Berman's reading of the *Manifesto* as a celebration of capitalism, it locates the distinctive temporal-political impulse of the text in its combination of the technique of historical montage with social scientific argument within the overarching performative unity and radically futural address of the manifesto as a rhetorical form.

Chapter Five pursues this dual theme of cultural-historical form and the de-historicizing moment of the political temporality of modernism – its wilful, abstract futurity – into the context of art criticism; specifically, the restrictions of Clement Greenberg's conception of modernist painting. Setting out from a discussion of the changing relationship between history and memory, it charts the contradictory potential of the de-historicizing function of aestheticization. Conceptual art was the first movement in the visual arts to attempt systematically to eliminate the aesthetic from artistic significance. In doing so, it enlisted the help of philosophy both to redefine the idea of the art work and to legitimate its new artistic strategies. Chapter Six analyses this unique conjunction in two ways: by deploying Bourdieu's conception of the field of cultural production to delineate the peculiar double-coding of philosophy as at once productive artistic material and legitimating discourse; and by offering an immanent analysis of the use of philosophical arguments in the critical writings and artistic self-conception of three major conceptual artists – Sol Lewitt, Joseph Kosuth, and the British group, Art & Language. Philosophy appears here simultaneously as ideal rational practice and itself a cultural-historical form.

Finally, Chapter Seven returns once again to the question of the forms of universality of general concepts in cultural theory, by raising the question of the ontological status of the concepts of psychoanalytical theory, in both their application within the analytical process and their use in cultural analysis. Taking as its object the metapsychological writings of the French psychoanalyst Jean Laplanche, unparalleled in their philosophical sophis-tication, it reconstructs the dynamic of ontological generalization and theoretical self-limitation inherent in the transposition of concepts from one context of application to another. In its development of a commu-nicational and translational paradigm of human relations, centred on the primacy of the opacity of the other, Laplanche's psychoanalytical theory also invokes the broader theme of the metaphysical basis of pragmatics. Ultimately, it is here, in the convergence of the thematics of post-Hegelian philosophy (history, politics, metaphysics) and cultural studies (significa-tion, practice, power) onto the concept of *experience* that the underlying unity of the book lies.

* * * * *

Chapter One, from which the book germinated, began life as an inau-gural lecture for a Professorship in Modern European Philosophy at Middlesex University in March 1999. Chapter Two grew, exponentially, from a paper written for the plenary panel, 'Uses of Benjamin', at the VIth Congress of the Brasilian Association for Comparative Literature (ABRALIC) in Florianopolis, August 1998. The original paper appears in a Portuguese translation in A.L. Andrade, M.L. de Barros Camarago, R. Antelo (eds.), *Leituras do Ciclo*, abralic/editora Grifos, Ilha de Santa Catarina, 1999. I am grateful to Raul Antelo for the invitation. An initial version of Chapter Three was presented to the conference 'Spectres of the West and the Politics of Translation' organized by *Traces* journal and the Chinese Academy of Social Sciences, Beijing, June 1999. I would like to thank Naoki Sakai for the invitation and the other participants in the conference for their comments on that text. The published version also appears in *Traces: A Multilingual Journal of Cultural Theory* no. 1 (2000).

The second and third sections of this chapter draw on a presentation to a panel on 'Modernism and National Culture' at the Mellon Sawyer Seminar on Cities and Nations, at the International Center for Advanced Studies, New York University, in November 1998. I am grateful to Harry Harootunian for the invitation and the participants in the seminar for their discussion of that draft. Chapter Four derives from talks to the conferences 'The Criticism of the Future', School of English, University of Kent, July 1997 and 'Social Emancipation: 150 Years After *The Communist Manifesto*', Cuban Academy of Social Sciences, Havana, February 1998. An earlier version appeared in *Socialist Register 1998: The Communist Manifesto Now*, edited by Leo Panitch and Colin Leys, Merlin Press, Rendlesham, 1998. Chapter Five was presented as a plenary paper to the 30th Congress of the International Association of Art Critics (AICA) in Rennes, August, 1996. Thanks to Jean-Marc Poinsot for the invitation. It first appeared in *Quelles Mémoires Pour L'Art Contemporain? Actes Du XXXe Congrès de l'Association Internationale des Critiques d'Art*, Presses Universitaire de Rennes, Rennes, 1997. Chapter Six had its distant origins in talks to the conferences 'Who's Afraid of Conceptual Art?' at the Institute of Contemporary Art, London, March 1996, and 'Healthy Alienation: Conceptual Art and Young British Art', Tate Gallery, London, June 1996. Its current, very different form was the result of a commission by Jon Bird and Michael Newman for their collection *Rethinking Conceptual Art*, Reaktion Books, London, 1999, to whom thanks are due for permission to use the material here. A preliminary version of Chapter Seven was presented to the conference 'Jean Laplanche: Explorations' at the Institute for Contemporary Arts, London, December 1999. I am indebted to Jean Laplanche for his response, which provoked the additional material included here.

Thanks to Howard Caygill for his comments, insightful as ever, on the initial proposal for the book. Special thanks for close readings of particular chapters are due to Francis Mulhern (who first suggested these essays might make a book), John Kraniauskas (who listened to or read them all in their original versions, and whose encouragement helped shape their final forms), Stella Sandford, John Fletcher and Lynne Segal, whose insistence that intellectual work make connections to broader cultural and political issues has been a model of critical practice, and upon whose support I depended throughout.

The MA in Modern European Philosophy and the MA in Visual Culture at Middlesex University provided the contrasting teaching contexts in which many of the ideas in the book were first expounded. I am grateful to the Center for the Critical Analysis of Contemporary Culture, Rutgers University, New Jersey, for providing me with a Research Fellowship in 1997–8 – and much to think about, especially about pragmatism – on its programme on 'The Aesthetic'. Thanks, in particular, for such a stimulating year to George Levine, Carolyn Williams, Elin Diamond and Xudong Zhang. This book is in many ways a by-product of that experience. The Middlesex University Research Committee NFFR fund provided me with the leave necessary to prepare the manuscript for publication.

In addition, I am grateful for kind permission by Nobuyoshi Araki and Araki Ltd for the use of his photograph as the cover image for this book.

1

PHILOSOPHY IN CULTURAL THEORY

What is the place of philosophy in cultural theory? The question appears straightforward, so straightforward in fact – so straightforwardly carto-graphical – as not actually to be a philosophical question at all. For what could be more routine, in principle at least, than surveying a particular field (cultural theory) for the signs of a particular kind of discourse (philosophy) in order to plot the path of its presence? But this is not my concern here, this mapping of the different philosophies at work in different forms of cultural theory, in different nationally specific institutional locations. Rather, my interest is at once more general, more specific, and more critical.

It is more general insofar as I am primarily concerned with the status and form of philosophical discourse *per se* within the field of cultural study, rather than with the reception of particular philosophies, less still particular philosophers; although the two cannot be wholly separated. It is more specific insofar as I am concerned with the theoretical trajectory of cultural studies in Britain and North America, from its origins in the post-imperial crisis of national identity in Britain in the 1950s to the trans-national aspirations of its more recent 'globalized' and internationally appropriated forms. Finally, what I have to say is, hopefully, more critical than a mere typology, in the broad Kantian sense of criticism, to the extent that it is concerned with the reflective demarcation of a field of legitimacy. In this case, what is the legitimate, appropriate and most productive role for specifically philosophical modes of thought in cultural theory today?

What role *could* and *should* philosophical thought play in cultural theory, were things to be as they might? This is another way of asking: how ought cultural theory to be (philosophically) today? Such a question is as much about cultural theory as it is about philosophy. To recognize this is to open out the original question – the role of philosophy in cultural theory – onto a much broader history: the troubled history of modern philosophy's relations with its non-philosophical others, its constitution by these relations, and consequently its not infrequently tortuous relations to itself. For in its Anglo-American development, cultural studies appears as one of philosophy's most stridently *non*-philosophical – indeed, proudly 'post-philosophical' – others. What is to be gained from an encounter between philosophy and so purportedly post-philosophical a field?

This chapter has five parts: a section on philosophy and non-philosophy – that is, on philosophical autonomy and disciplinarity; an account of theory in the constitution of cultural studies; a brief discussion of pragmatism; further remarks on the relationship between 'use' and 'truth'; and a concluding section on those features of cultural theory – totalization, generality and abstraction – that point towards a philosophical interpretation of its most general concepts. In each instance, I offer a snapshot of a broad, occasionally sweeping view: a condensation, a simplification, a vignette. This series of stills carries with it an argument of its own.

Philosophy and non-philosophy

It is a defining characteristic of Western philosophy since Kant that it has been preoccupied by the need to justify itself as a distinct and self-sufficient form of intellectual activity or 'discipline', while nonetheless retaining a connection to the forms of universality characteristic of its more expansive, intellectually promiscuous past, in which 'philosophy' was synonymous with theoretical knowledge in general – the terminological distinction between philosophy and the sciences being the product of the late eighteenth century, no earlier. This process of self-justification has been an anxious, contradictory and crisis-ridden affair, lurching wildly between bloated self-importance and annihilating self-depreciation, in which, as the last century progressed, professional philosophy was often reduced to narrowing down its justification to exist to its unique ability to demonstrate that it has, in fact, no right to exist, at least as previously practised and understood in the modern period: that is, as a discipline of the universality of autonomous reason. (I take this as a broad working definition of modern philosophy: the discipline of the universality of autonomous reason, which is also therefore necessarily a form of self-discipline, a discipline of the rational self.) Philosophy's sole consolation in such cases has been that this demonstration must be ongoing, must continue piecemeal, *ad infinitum*, philosophical utterance by philosophical utterance, if it is not to become self-refutingly generalized: a definitive result of the universality of autonomous reason.[1] In such instances, philosophy lives on only negatively, yet nonetheless secure in the piecemeal character of its scepticism about itself. Such is the affinity between the late Wittgenstein and a certain practice of deconstruction, for example, marked out by Rorty, who acts here, as elsewhere, as a point of indifference between the two traditions. Thus, over the last fifty years, the stripped down, shiny new, early-century professionalisms of analytical philosophy and Husserlian phenomenology – the Anglo-American and 'continental' versions of philosophy as an independent 'science' – have been subjected to corrosive contextualist, deconstructive and pragmatist critiques, alike.

Philosophy as the philosophical critique of the idea of philosophy as an independent science was the dominant metaphilosophical tendency in the twentieth century in both European and North American professional philosophy. As MacIntyre once put it, *à propos* of Rorty: epitaph-writing has for some time now been working its way up the list of accepted professional activities.[2] Yet this internalist, self-annihilating mode of philosophical reflection is by no means the only, or indeed the primary, way in which the idea of the universality of autonomous reason has been undermined in the period since Kant. Far from it. In fact, one might view all this as being no more than a reaction-formation, in the Freudian sense, in which the repressed desire to continue doing philosophy in the bad old way (as a discipline of the universality of autonomous reason) manifests itself only through the counter-cathexis of a will to end it, leading – as is usual in such cases – to a result directly opposite to the one consciously intended: namely, the continuation of philosophy as an autonomous discipline, albeit in ever more rarefied forms of self-negation. As a reaction-formation, the philosophical critique of philosophy possesses a symptomatic value which suggests that we look more deeply into the motives governing the necessity for the repression of the original desire: the desire to carry on philosophizing. When we do this, it quickly becomes clear that it is the internalization of externally imposed constraints on the universality of philosophical reason that underlies and motivates the profound ambivalence characteristic of twentieth-century European and North American philosophy's relationship to itself.

Two such constraints stand out as being of most general significance: the rapid growth in the independent cultural authority of the empirical sciences from the latter half of the eighteenth century onwards (and of literary study during the course of the twentieth century); and the failure of the world either to be or to become 'philosophical', in the sense of the various philosophies of the future which flourished in the wake of Hegelianism in the second half of the nineteenth century, foremost amongst which are those of Marx and Nietzsche. It was the first of these constraints that led to the self-imposed ban on philosophy's claim on empirical object-domains, its restriction to merely corrective forms of logical and methodological (later, linguistic) self-reflection on pre-given conceptual structures, and thereby, the crisis in the very idea of philosophy as an independent discipline, which continues today. The effects of the second, practical-political or more broadly historical constraint – what I have called the failure of the world to 'become philosophical' – have been more ambiguous, since this failure fuels the very need, the need for philosophy, that it simultaneously frustrates. There is thus a disjunctive relationship between the two constraints. Something of the character of this disjunction

– a disjunction between the theoretical and practical functions of philosophy as a discipline of the universality of autonomous reason – can be gauged from its presence within the Kantian problematic itself.

When Kant first deployed the strategy of restricting the legitimate domain of the theoretical use of pure reason as the means for *strengthening* the claim for its 'control' over other disciplines, within that restricted domain, it was the traditionally defined 'higher', governmentally regulated, university faculties of theology, law and medicine with which his philosophy was thrown into conflict, as recounted in his book *The Conflict of the Faculties*.[3] What Kant describes there as 'the department of historical knowledge (including history, geography, philology and the humanities, along with all the empirical knowledge contained in the natural sciences)' was still considered part of philosophy, alongside the department of 'pure rational knowledge', which is what we are more likely to think of as 'philosophy' today, in its modern disciplinary sense. These two departments were united by Kant in the name of *truth* (which he describes as 'the essential and first condition of learning in general') in opposition to the mere *utility* to the government of the so-called higher faculties.[4] Philosophy was thus actually the highest faculty for Kant, speaking 'pure intellectually', and within it, it is pure rational knowledge which reigns supreme, since its concepts constitute the very form – albeit not the particular content – of the 'experience' upon which historical knowledge is based.

Soon, however, as the metaphysical implications of Kant's transcendental philosophy became increasingly evident, in the subsequent development of German idealism, a new conflict of the faculties arose *internal* to Kant's faculty of philosophy between the department of 'historical knowledge' (or what we would now call the sciences and the humanities), on the one hand, and the residual claims to conceptual legislation maintained by the department of 'pure rational knowledge' (or what we would now think of as 'philosophy' proper), on the other. This was a contest which pure rational knowledge could not ultimately win (even in its dialectically appropriative Hegelian form) because of the rapidly historically changing character and increasing social utility of the empirical sciences themselves. But neither, it seems, could it be decisively defeated, so long as it included a conception of *the future* among its privileged objects. In fact, it was in defence of a strictly philosophical claim on the future that Kant had felt impelled to write *The Conflict of the Faculties* in the first place.

Kant's intervention into the politics of the Prussian university system was provoked by the subjection of his book *Religion Within the Limits of Mere Reason* to the department of biblical theology within the Censorship Commission in Berlin, in 1791, which forbade its publication. The first part, which had been sent to the philosophy censor, had been approved. Politically, *The Conflict of the Faculties* is thus essentially a book about censorship. Indeed, it is the founding text of the modern concept of academic freedom, with all the qualifications such a notion implies. However, this political dimension has its roots in a philosophical debate about *the mode of determination of our relationship to the future*: in this case, rational versus biblical theology. (The political significance of biblical theology for the state derived from its franchise on the future.) Famously, Kant subjected the domain of pure philosophy to a three-fold division, by the questions 'what can I know?', 'what ought I to do?', and 'what can I hope?' As his thought developed, the ground of pure reason's self-justification moved successively from one domain to the next: from *knowledge* to *action* to *speculation*. It is the philosophy of religion, rational theology (religion within the bounds of mere reason), which regulates the third domain and is thus the intellectual arbiter of hope. The philosophical discourse of modernity – the historical ontology of the present – thus finds its highest expression in Kant in the role of rational theology in regulating the structure of the philosophy of history.

It was on this terrain, the terrain of the philosophy of history, that what we might call the *first endgame* of philosophy was played out in the middle of the nineteenth century, in the wake of Hegel's death, in Marx's early writings, in the dual form of 1) the epistemological critique of the speculative dialectic (the claim that absolute idealism ultimately abolishes time) and 2) the project for the actualization of the alienated universality of philosophical reason through a politics (communism) with world-historical aspirations. Kant's claim on the future was displaced by Marx from philosophy to politics; but politics was at the same time mortgaged to the positive sciences. A gap thus opened up between the epistemological critique of speculation and its practical significance as the theoretical ground for thinking the future. The question became: what happens to the status of specifically philosophical – that is, speculatively totalizing – reason in the historical disjunction between the two sides of its critique? It is this same question that Adorno raised once again in the 1960s, in the wake of the failure of historical communism. In the words of the famous opening line of *Negative Dialectics*, philosophy 'lives on because the moment to realize it was missed'.[5] But in what form, precisely? This remains the question today. The question is not so much 'Why still philosophy?' (although this is Rorty's question – and the title of a well-known radio lecture by Adorno from 1962),[6] but rather, 'How still philosophy?' How still philosophy *despite*, or in the face of, the epistemological critique of speculation. This has been the abiding preoccupation of (non-analytical) European philosophy since the 1840s.

In short, if European philosophy achieved disciplinary autonomy on the basis of its limitation of the theoretical claims of pure reason, its main traditions nonetheless continue to assert its right to exist as a search for truth, in the face of the ongoing critique of even its most limited claims to knowledge, on the basis of the practical – social and existential – significance of its speculative dimension: transcendence of the given, thought beyond experience, or the idea of a qualitatively better future; be that in the Hegelian form of a search for reconciliation (Novalis's 'urge to be at home everywhere'), a Marxist politics of communism, a Nietzschean will to power ('Where is – *my* home? I ask and seek and have sought it; I have not found it'), or an existentialist quest for authenticity – to mention only the most prominent varieties. However, if this right is accepted, in whatever form, it reacts back on the epistemological critique of claims to totality, modifying it decisively. 'One *cannot not* think the whole, however problematically', thus remains the main lesson of Kant's philosophy, although it requires a rather different defence from the one Kant used to argue for the necessity of regulative ideas.[7] In its orientation towards reflection on a *speculative inter-disciplinarity of empirical knowledges*, this is not a message that professional, disciplinary philosophy in the Anglo-American tradition has been eager to hear.

There has been an increasing disjunction, since the death of Hegel, between the theoretical self-limitation of philosophy as a professional activity and the broader cultural functions of self-knowledge and the provision of coherence in the totality of experience (including, necessarily, expectations about the future) through which the classical vocation of philosophy as a mode of life (indeed, allegedly the highest mode, the philosophical life) has been carried forward, transformed, into the modern world. This disjunction is expressed in two radically different notions of philosophical universality: one, *disciplinary* and merely logical or methodological in form; the other, *anti-disciplinary*, substantive, historical, and inherently speculative. However, paradoxically, for all its prospective *inter*-disciplinarity, this latter, *anti*-disciplinary, speculative form of universality cannot but appear alongside the preconstituted disciplines – including the narrow variant of philosophy itself – as an *anti-disciplinary specialism*, excessive in relation to each and every disciplinary field, yet without a determinate field of its own. This paradoxical, primarily critical role – analogous to the place of aesthetic judgement within Kant's system[8] – remains, I shall suggest, the most productive role for philosophy today. In this role, philosophy discloses a secret affinity with one of its most determinedly non-philosophical others: contemporary cultural studies.

Theory in cultural studies

One need not be a specialist in cultural studies in Britain to know that its formative impulses ran against the grain, not merely of the structure of university disciplines in the late 1950s and 1960s, but of the prevailing forms of the institutionalization of knowledge more generally. Nor need one be an expert to know that its guiding light here was political, or more broadly, political-educational – 'a political project of popular educa-tion' as one recent commentator describes it[9] – rather than philosophical. Indeed, philosophy is one of the very few disciplines in the humanities and social sciences which seems to have had no influence on the forma-tion of cultural studies in Britain (as Stuart Hall has recently confirmed[10]); except perhaps implicitly and negatively, as a prefigurative warning about the potentially conservative implications of the otherwise democratic connotations of the word 'ordinary'. Culture, for Raymond Williams was, famously, 'ordinary'; but so, allegedly, was the kind of philosophy prac-tised by J.L. Austin at Oxford in the 1950s: ordinary language philosophy. As the 1960s progressed, the warning became clear. Soon it would be *sub*-cultures which would be ordinary, or better, 'popular'. The alleged ordinariness of Williams's 'common culture' would begin to look as ideo-logically loaded as the language of Austin's Oxford common room.[11]

Nonetheless, for all the uselessness to early cultural studies of the nation-ally prevailing form of philosophical thought in Britain in the 1950s and 1960s – a culturally restricted, disciplinary version of logico-linguistic analysis – there are two striking parallels between the intellectual struc-ture of cultural studies as a political project of popular education and cultural democratization, and the anti-disciplinary variant of a certain form of post-Hegelian philosophical thought and cultural analysis, repre-sented paradigmatically by the Institute for Social Research, Frankfurt: the project of critical theory. These are:

1) their common paradoxical status as *anti-disciplinary specialisms*, or specialisms in a *cross-disciplinary type of generality*;
2) the connection of this totalizing impulse of cross-disciplinary gener-ality – for it is precisely that, whether it be Williams's 'whole way of life', Althusser's 'decentred structure in dominance', or Bhabha's 'culture as difference' – to a specific form of practice, namely, polit-ics, in its extended modern sense, as the constitution of the social *per se*: a willed ordering and reordering – production, reproduction and transformation – of the ensemble of social relations.

The Frankfurt critical theorists themselves, notoriously, failed to make the transition from a negatively totalizing form of interdisciplinary research and analysis to the political thinking it was supposed to inform; in large part, because of the suffocating effects of the category of instrumental reason, which increasingly supervened on the specificities of interdisciplin-ary research itself. With the honourable exception of Marcuse during the 1960s and 1970s, they showed no inclination to engage with the con-ditions and cultural representations of marginal and subordinate groups, or to associate with social movements or political groups.[12] Nor despite their reputation within the Marxist tradition for both modernism and 'culturalism', did they make much headway in producing a differentiated analysis of the new cultural forms of post-war capitalism. However, in its original formulation, critical theory was not actually a variant of 'cultural studies' at all – for which there was no equivalent in the German-speaking world, where the relations between disciplines has a different history, until very recently, in Berlin, where the term *Kulturwissenschaften* (cultural sciences) has begun to be used in a comparable manner. Rather, critical theory was a cross-disciplinary theory of society, modelled on and grounded in Marx's critique of political economy, which worked philosophy, sociology and psychoanalytical psychology into a hypothetical and counterfactually totalizing view. It did not accept the term 'culture' as the name for this totality; although it did approach what would become cultural studies through its practice of ideology-critique.[13] However, the restriction of its account of the social form of subjectivity to the parameters of Marx's theory of value – generalized through the notion of the culture industry – combined with an orthodox, ahistorical Freudianism, made it largely indifferent to the specificities of the emergent cultural forms.

In this regard, the brilliant particularity and trenchant judgements of Adorno's post-war cultural criticism appear as compensatory supplements to, and diversions from, theoretical deficiencies which they both disguise and reproduce. Formally, at least, these writings derive from another tradition: the Nietzschean lineage of *Kulturkritik* for which the particularity of the object of criticism demands a corresponding individuality of both judgement and critical form, in what is effectively a cultural-historical generalization of Kantian aesthetic. Adorno drew upon the conceptual resources of a Marxian reading of classical German philosophy in his critical fragments and essays, but he eschewed lower level historical concepts, preferring instead to mediate the individual cultural object *directly* with the highest levels of universality (subject/object, freedom/unfreedom, commodity-form). This both made these philosophical universals 'live' and imparted often breathtaking emblematic significance to particular cultural phenomena. However, for all their particularity – indeed, as a consequence of a certain over-particularization – these writings avoid theoretical specification of the social relations constitutive of different cultural practices and forms. Thus, while critical theory achieved impressive levels of sophistication in the theoretical self-understanding of its project as a negatively totalizing cross-disciplinary form (not least in Adorno's philosophical writings of the 1960s), it failed to carry that project through at a sufficiently concrete, historically and geo-politically differentiated, theoretical level.

Post-war cultural studies in Britain and North America, on the other hand, was grounded in a strong sense of cultural differentiation and change and of the contradictory democratic potential of emergent new commercial forms. However, the theoretical implications of the totalizing structure of its educational-political project have been largely neglected.[14] It remains unclear what happens to its totalizing impulse when one acknowledges the radical openness of the historical process, on the one hand, and the increasing implausibility of restricting its spatial dimension to national-political forms of territoriality, on the other; or how the meaning of the various lower-level categories of cultural experience, which constitute the body of cultural theory, is affected by their location within such an open-ended and spatially diffused totalizing process. Yet these have been the key theoretical issues for systematically-oriented European philosophy since the death of Hegel. (Systematically-*oriented* philosophy, that is, which is a far broader category than philosophy which is systematic in presentational form, since it includes its obverse, anti-systematic philosophy – systematically anti-systematic philosophy – as the line of thought which runs from early Romanticism, via Nietzsche to Benjamin and Adorno, or F.R. Leavis, shows.) There is thus considerable theoretical scope for exchange between the two traditions – systematically-oriented post-Kantian philosophy and cultural studies – despite the antagonisms which have characterized their relationship to date.

Yet, at the level of its theoretical self-consciousness, cultural studies has tended increasingly towards an *anti*-totalizing, conjuncturalist pragmatism as its privileged mode (even when dealing with issues such as 'globalization'); and it has done so, more often than not, as a matter of principled theoretical-political pride, rather than as an acknowledgement of the pressures imposed upon its practice by the changing institutional and political configurations of the 1980s and 1990s. Even at its most explicitly totalizing, in Fredric Jameson's theorization of postmodernism as a cultural dominant, for example, the mode of theory-construction ('transcoding') is self-consciously 'post-philosophical' or pragmatic in form. It proceeds through the piecemeal appropriation of displaced fragments of the philosophical tradition, in a practice of syncretic agglomeration and *bricolage*, which eschews all systematic (or any rigorously anti-systematic) logic.[15] Yet pragmatism is itself a philosophical position. In fact, it is the overwhelmingly dominant theoretical mode across the humanities in both the United States (its home) and increasingly, albeit less self-consciously, in Britain and elsewhere.

Pragmatism is the philosophical unconscious of post-Marxist cultural studies. More specifically, it is that mode of the philosophical critique of philosophy through which contemporary cultural study distances itself from the systematic and metaphysical perspectives of post-Kantian philosophical thought. In this respect, cultural theory is always already philosophical, even in its most anti-philosophical modes. If there is an epistemological break or rupture between German idealism and Anglo-American cultural studies – a radical theoretical incommensurability – consequent upon the disintegration of the intellectual culture of Marxism, their original mediating link, then it is 'pragmatism', rather than 'science', that is the sign of this break (Sidney Hook its ironic precursor). *Marxism is the vanishing mediator in the formation of cultural studies.* More or less all that is left of it in contemporary cultural studies is a desire for relevance which, as intense as it is abstract, takes on an increasingly prag-matic form.[16] Any argument regarding the value to contemporary cultural theory of the conceptual resources of the systematic and metaphysical side of post-Kantian philosophical thought must thus pass through the critique of pragmatism as a philosophical position.

Pragmatism

As a consciously articulated philosophical position, pragmatism is a rela-tively recent phenomenon. It is conventionally dated to a paper by the American philosopher Charles Sanders Peirce published in two parts in 1877/8 entitled 'How to Make our Ideas Clear'. In this paper, Peirce formulates what he called 'a rule for attaining the third grade of clearness of apprehension': namely, 'Consider what effects, which might conceivably have practical bearings, we conceive the object of our conception to have. Then our conception of these effects is the whole of our conception of the object.'[17] For Peirce, pragmatism was the theory that a conception ('the rational purport of a word') 'lies exclusively in its conceivable bearing upon the conduct of life'.[18] There are three things to note about this def-inition. First, it occupies a specific domain within the theory of meaning. Pragmatism for Peirce is a theory of the *rational* meaning of *intellectual* concepts, not a theory of meaning as such. Second, it refers us to the domain of *conceivable* rather than merely *actual* effects. Rational meaning belongs to the domain of virtuality, imaginative possibility, not mere actuality. And third, it is not an account of truth. Pierce continued to uphold a correspondence theory of truth. The 'constraint of reality' grounds his projection of ultimate agreement between investigators in a speculatively inferred future. The now more familiar idea of Apel and Habermas of an 'ideal speech situation', transcendentalizes this moment of agreement, converts Peirce's correspondence theory into a consensus theory of truth, and thereby robs Peircean pragmatics of its speculative metaphysical realism.[19]

Clearly, the pragmatism of the mainstream of contemporary cultural the-ory is decidedly un-Peircean, although there has been sporadic and uneven interest in Peirce's semiotics since the 1960s (for a discussion of which, see the next chapter). If there are cultural theorists who are philosophically close to Peirce, they are the unlikely pair of Walter Benjamin and Gilles Deleuze, whose positions increasingly appear affiliated these days, in their respective metaphysical radicalisms. There is a 'minor' pragmatist tradition – a metaphysical pragmatism of the image – which runs from Nietzsche, via Peirce, into Benjamin and Deleuze. However, insofar as it has a theoretically identifiable form, the pragmatism of contemporary cultural theory is closer to that of Rorty's reception of William James and John Dewey, who were the first to convert Peirce's logic of inquiry into a theory about truth. More specifically, James and Dewey deployed the idea of use (Peirce's 'practical bearings') to *dissolve* the metaphysical dimension of the concept of truth. As James put it in *Pragmatism* (1907): 'ideas . . . *become* true just so far as they help us to get into satisfactory relations with other parts of our experience'. Hence his famous definition: 'the true is the name of whatever *proves itself to be good* in the way of belief', subsequently glossed, notoriously, as the 'cash-value' of experience.[20]

This shift from a speculative experimental theory of the rational meaning of intellectual concepts (Peirce) to a reduction of truth to use (James and Dewey) is well known.[21] Less often noted, however, is the way in which the temporal range, and hence the political meaning, of the theory is transformed as a result of the elimination of its metaphysical dimension. From the standpoint of knowledge, metaphysical pragmatism distinguishes itself from non-metaphysical pragmatism by the depth of its temporal horizon. Truth must be secured against the future, or to put it the other way around: metaphysical realism requires the standpoint of the end of time. And there is not much 'cash-value' there. (Classically, philosophy has always been associated with the standpoint of death.) This is a position that is maintained in a not dissimilar (non-Hegelian) form by Walter Benjamin. However, unlike Peirce and Benjamin, who retain a speculative historical dimension to inquiry, James reduces the philosophical meaning of the future to the 'definite difference . . . [a particular view] will make to you or me, at definite instants of our life'.[22] Future generations need not apply. This positivistic emphasis on the empirically demonstrable yields a 'presentism' (an exclusive emphasis on the temporal horizon of the historical present, over and against those of past and future), which has little regard for the futural dimension of historical thought: that is, for the qualitatively new. It is consequently antagonistic to any politics which is grounded there: that is, to any politics which is not essentially conservative, in the Burkean sense.

What the James-Dewey line of pragmatism offers cultural theory is, first, a strong sense of relevance, even urgency, as an epistemological criterion (things must be expressed in practical consequences in the present if they are to be judged true); and second, a philosophical legitimation for its neglect of the systematic conceptual constraints at stake in the metaphysical tradition of European philosophy, and in particular for its retreat from 'history', in the philosophical sense. This lack of a philosophical concept of history is connected to a further, more familiar issue which bedevils pragmatism as a theory of truth: the indeterminacy of its constitutive subject or the problem of the 'us'. However, just as what I have diagnosed as the philosophical fault of pragmatism's 'presentism' (the positivism of its temporal

11

horizon) is precisely part of its appeal to contemporary cultural theory, with its insistence on immediate and practically demonstrable relevance, so too that appeal lies in the indeterminacy of its constitutive subject. This offers space for an indifferent empirical plurality of competing subject-positions ('identities'), and hence a plurality of pragmatic 'truths'. Its philosophical weaknesses are its precise practical attraction. Within the terms of its temporal constraints, pragmatism is politically indeterminate, since politics is premised on fundamental *disagreement* about what 'proves itself to be good' in the way of belief.[23] The consequences of this indeterminacy went largely unrecognized by James and Dewey on account of their humanism: their presupposition of broad agreement about what will 'prove itself to be good'. They thus underestimated the potential within pragmatism as a philosophical position for politics to determine epistemology, or more commonly these days, for 'culture' to do so, since the inherent plurality of the political is now frequently reduced to a manifestation, rather than a mediating cause, of cultural difference ('multiculturalism'). In such cases, 'culture' is in danger of taking the political out of politics, in the very act of becoming its privileged mode.

Thus, if truth is to be reduced to 'whatever proves itself to be good in the way of belief', in the present, the questions arise, 'good for whom?' and 'for what purposes?' Just how much epistemological virtue one finds in Rorty's version of 'solidarity', for example – the solidarity of 'us bourgeois postmodern liberals', in his notorious phrase[24] – will depend upon who you are and what you have to live with. It is the lower-level cultural contextualism which is implied in these phrases, when they are interpreted within the restricted temporal horizon of a conjuncturalist present, that structures the pragmatism of the main theoretical line of cultural studies today and serves as the basis for its politics. The concrete is reduced to the conjunctural; the conjunctural is reduced to the contingent. Politics becomes the enactment of a semiotic version of a Nietzschean voluntarism.[25] For presentism, the epistemological impatience inherent in non-metaphysical pragmatism, is equally – indeed, more intensely – to be found in the seemingly more radically futural case of Nietzsche. Nietzsche's *Uses and Disadvantages of History for Life* predates the publication of Peirce's founding essay by four years, but it remains the most sophisticated example of a radically pragmatist approach to historical thought. There is futurity here, for sure, but the future is wholly beholden to the will constitutive of individual action in the present. There is no history (*Geschichte*) in the sense of actual history, a practically enacted, socially embedded transgenerational narrative intelligibility which closes off, as much as it opens up – indeed, opens up by virtue of the way in which it also closes off – specific futures. There are just epistemologically indifferent modes of historical representation (*Historie*) of varying 'uses and disadvantages' for an abstractly specified 'life'.[26]

The convenience of non-metaphysical pragmatism as a (post-)philosophical position is that it leaves your lower level theory exactly as it finds it. Pragmatism abdicates from the vocation of modern philosophy as critique. Everything comes to depend upon 'what is good' in the present, but the structure of possibilities and probabilities making up the present is never totalized, theoretically, however hypothetically, since the standpoint of totalization has been vacated. It is here that the systematic and metaphysical tradition of post-Kantian European philosophy – which is also the systematically anti-systematic tradition of post-Kantian European philosophy – has resources to offer, if it can break free from its predominantly scholastic reception in North America and Britain as a primarily philological and interpretive mode of disciplinary – that is, conceptually self-sufficient – philosophical practice. For despite the constrictions of its presentism, the focus of cultural studies on present practices (cultural study as a study of the present) is a vital corrective to the scholasticism of most disciplinary philosophy – the recent turn to 'ethics' and 'the political' in Anglo-American continental philosophy notwithstanding. To develop as a living tradition, post-Kantian European philosophy must engage with the determinate conceptual content and current practices of other disciplines within the humanities and social sciences: that is, it must put its concepts to use. But is this not to capitulate to the very pragmatism I have been criticizing, to make philosophy's 'usefulness' the criterion of its truth? To counter this charge, and to develop the argument further, it is necessary to say something, however brief, about the relationship of use to truth.

Use, truth and history

Nietzsche's *Uses and Disadvantages of History for Life* is a philosophical source for the radical presentism of non-metaphysical pragmatist thought. It was also of foundational significance for Walter Benjamin's attempt to develop a political historiography of modernity on the basis of a metaphysical conception of historical time. This conjunction hints at the depths which lurk beneath the surface of the idea of use. It is a central feature of Benjamin's thought that in certain respects it resists 'use' (the functional adaption to pre-given ends – its use by cultural studies, for example) as firmly as its methodological dictum on the necessity to tear historical objects out of their contexts in order 'to *cite* history' demands it.[27] Hence the peculiar status of quotations from Benjamin's writings in so many contemporary cultural studies: suspended as self-sufficient insights – gem-like truths, strangers – within discourses that are foreign to them. This is in part a product of Benjamin's style, midway between aphorism, fragment and montage. Yet for Benjamin (as for Adorno) form is part of the truth-content of a work. The maintenance of a metaphysical conception of truth immeasurably complicates the idea of use. Truth, for Benjamin, is historical, but it is historical in a far deeper and more difficult sense than knowledge is. Benjamin's approach to the historical character of truth provides a model of how the standpoint of totalization can be critically maintained in the light of the radical openness of the historical process, through the construction of a dialectic of use and truth.

If by the historicity of knowledge we understand the relativity of all knowledge to its historical present, then such an idea is not only compatible with a certain pragmatism, it requires it. As Nietzsche argued, criticism of a representational conception of truth (what Benjamin called truth as 'known truth') from the standpoint of an anthropological materialism (the bio-social dynamics of human life), leads inexorably to the priority of 'use' over 'truth' in the notion of knowledge.[28] For Benjamin, contra Hegel, '[t]ruth and knowledge are never identical; there is no true knowledge and no known truth'.[29] Rather, precisely because knowledge is historical, and hence relative, however systematically it is aggregated, truth, which in its classical metaphysical sense is absolute, can only be conceived from the standpoint of history as a fulfilled whole. However, this standpoint is not available (since the future has yet to occur), except speculatively, through the mediation of experience by the *idea* of history as a completed or fulfilled whole. Experience of truth ('true experience') thus always involves claims on the future (the collective future), as well as of knowledge. Benjamin writes speculative cultural history. On this view, historical experience has a practical dimension derived from the eschatological concept of fulfillment (justice), which modifies or inflects the pragmatic dimension of the claims to knowledge to which it is connected. In this respect, its objects have a 'revolutionary' use-value derived, precisely, from their *redemption* from use in the immediate, positivistic sense in which 'use' is understood in the James-Dewey strand of the pragmatist tradition. Constituted through use, epistemologically speaking, their truth is nonetheless tied up with the standpoint of the end of time.[30] Such experiences are, for Benjamin, necessarily imagistic, since only in the spatial wholeness of the image can the wholeness of history be figured as a form of speculative experience. 'Wholeness' is Benjamin's image of the image; metonymy, the figural basis of his historical thought.[31]

Benjamin thus constructs a speculative dialectic of truth and use in which the radically temporalizing force of Nietzsche's anti-Platonism – the productivism of his active nihilism, so familiar in contemporary theory – is tempered by the formal idealism of an atemporal eternity.[32] 'Truth is the death of intention.'[33] Benjamin's imagistic conception of historical experience mediates these extremes of movement and stasis, in a non-Hegelian logical form. To put it in perhaps not inappropriately Kantian terms: in Benjamin, the idea of truth (history as a fulfilled whole) *regulates* construction and interpretation alike, replacing the quasi-biological framework of Nietzsche's 'life' with a historical view, from which the futurity bottled up in a variety of outmoded historical objects and practices may be experienced in the 'specific legibility' of the relations between their 'then' and the 'now'. (Such objects need to be outmoded, or separated from their practical functions within the present, in order that they may be 'quoted' as history. This is the indexical realism of Benjamin's conception of history, the photographic basis of his historical thought.) The practicalities of the present are constitutive – 'The events surrounding the historian, and in which he himself takes part, will underlie his presentation in the form of a text written in invisible ink'[34] – but they enable, rather than prohibit, a relation to truth. This is not a utopian standpoint, since it does not project fulfillment into another place or a later historical time. Rather, it reconfigures the dialectic of the then and the now within the present, from the standpoint of an exteriority beyond time. Concrete as it is, it is in no way 'concretely utopian' in the Blochean sense, since Benjamin rejected Bloch's form of messianic identification of actually existing political forces.

It is the horizon of anticipation constructed by this idea of truth, the famous messianic moment – rather than simply 'the present' either in Nietzsche's ultimately eternalizing or in some more everyday (chronological or conjunctural) sense – which determines the practical moment of Benjamin's thought. A 'messianic' view of the future constitutes the historical meaning of the present, as surely as (in line with Nietzsche's account) the practicalities of the present constitute the historical meaning of the past, which opens up its relations to the future, in turn. Thus, when Benjamin writes that '[p]olitics attains primacy over history',[35] we should remember that his understanding of politics derives from a Romantic, metaphorically displaced theological historical view – 'the desire to realize the kingdom of God on earth', as he quotes Schlegel's description of 'the inception of modern history' in his dissertation on Romanticism (1920)[36] – while 'history' refers here to the backward-looking, reconstructive view of the traditional historian. For the materialist historian, politics is constitutive of history (attains primacy *within* history), in its proper philosophical sense.

The question of use is thus philosophically more tricky than certain of Benjamin's own more productivist pronouncements might lead us to suppose. In an intellectual climate dominated by pragmatic attitudes to theory and an all-too-easy presentism – in which the metaphysical dimension of Benjamin's concept of experience is perceived as a distinct 'disadvantage' and actively forgotten – it is, paradoxically, in its moment of resistance to certain uses (the bolstering of pragmatism, for example), that the best use of Benjamin's thought is to be made.

To value the systematic and metaphysical resources of post-Kantian philosophy for their prospective uses in cultural theory, then, is not necessarily to be complicit in the reduction of truth to use. It is merely to draw attention to the distinctive theoretical and political use-values immanent in the metaphysical conception of truth, from which Benjamin derives an historical conception of use. This conception of use constitutes a distinctive version of the philosophical discourse of modernity, in the Foucauldian sense of an ontology of the historical present. (Modernity is the paradigmatic form of post-Hegelian concepts of history; post-modernity, its fading shadow.) Such a discourse carries with it the imperative, unearthed by Adorno in the writing of the French poet Rimbaud, 'to be absolutely modern':[37] that is, to totalize the historical present, absolutely. For only thus can one be sure that one's philosophical concepts are living forms, totalizing and hence re-temporalizing mediations of positive concepts – of cultural theory, among other domains. (Self-sufficient philosophy is vampiric: it lives off the positive concepts it disavows.) Moreover, only those positive concepts which have been thus mediated will be analytically adequate to action on a par with the educational-political project from which cultural studies set out; which is not to say that such action will therefore be practically adequate, since the speculative character of such mediations reflects the necessarily experimental character of historical action. But it will be projected on an appropriate historical scale. A preliminary specification of the theoretical terms of such mediations can be gleaned from the distinctive forms of *totalization, generality* and *abstraction* associated with the idea of philosophy and cultural theory as speculative anti- and cross-disciplinary specialisms. These forms will be elaborated further with reference to particular concepts in the chapters that follow.

Totalization, generality, abstraction

Cultural studies, I have argued, has a totalizing trajectory that flows from its educational-political project, however fervently it may have come to reject totalization, formally, as a conceptual procedure. This rejection derives, first, from a restrictively Hegelian conception of totalization as a philosophical form, and second, from the 'ethnic absolutism' implicit in its presumed spatial ground: the territoriality of the nation-state. Outside of this context, however, there are several different ways of defending totalization philosophically – several different philosophical forms of totalization – and various more concrete reasons why cultural theorists might take the philosophical dynamics and difficulties of totalization (and de-totalization) more seriously than they currently do. I have discussed three such philosophical forms in detail, elsewhere. I shall not repeat that argument here.[38] Suffice to say: (1) that the question of totalization is essentially a question of the unity of temporalizations; (2) that this question arises at four distinct ontological levels or dimensions (human individuals, nature, social forms, and history); (3) that 'history' is the ongoing, imperfect narrative mediation of the other three dimensions; (4) that the concept of modernity functions at the level of the temporalization of history itself. These are the philosophical presuppositions of what follows. As such they provide a broad analytical framework for reflection on the meanings of more concrete but nonetheless still general concepts which act as mediating unities across the disciplinary fields through which the ontological domains listed above are parceled out for study. General concepts in cultural theory are mediating cross-disciplinary concepts of this type. As such, they construct the objects of contemporary cultural study as universal in their potential social meanings and global in their potential spatial reach – as the economic, technological and political logics which structure contemporary cultural exchanges have indeed become.[39] There is no spatial limit to the social, below the level of the planetary, here.

This gives rise to the necessity to think the temporal dimension of this new form of socio-spatial totality in a unified way – i.e. to return to the terrain of philosophical concepts of history, from the standpoint of the spatio-temporal dynamics of the current state of the global system. In this respect, philosophical defences of totalization converge with conceptual demands internal to the development of the object-domain of cultural studies itself. However, this is not to say that globality is the only legitimate spatial basis for totalization, but rather that it is its ultimate horizon. Study of particular objects will always require lower-level (less inclusive) totalizations as their spatial bases. Such totalizations will, however, nonetheless, if only implicitly, refer beyond themselves to more inclusive processes, up to the speculative levels of world history and, ultimately, natural history, which will refigure their conceptual form. Conversely, methodologically *a priori* as such 'absolute' totalization is, it will be an empty formalism outside of its ongoing, hypothetical and defeasible construction as the relational totality of lower-level totalizations, the meanings of which will be transformed in the process. Such is the virtuous hermeneutical circularity of a post-Hegelian dialectical logic. Paul Gilroy's concept of the 'black Atlantic' is an example of the construction of a new lower-level socio-geographic basis for the totalization of a particular object (the experience of black people in contemporary Britain), in the wake of the criticism of a previous, more restricted form (the nation-state and its imperial extensions). As such, it refigures its object of study via new conceptual terms.[40] Different objects of study, within the same empirical space, will require different primary levels of socio-spatial totalization (locale, province, nation, federation, region, space of flows) which will subsequently require mediation at other levels. Hence the potential structural disjunctions between, for example, the economic, political and cultural histories of any particular territoriality. Totalization is a re-territorializing as well as a re-temporalizing process.

17

A speculative anti-disciplinary form of philosophical universality is thus at the same time, necessarily, a cross-disciplinary type of generality, which, by virtue of its refiguration of relations between disciplinary object-domains, acts as a critically mediating form. It is a distinctive feature of concepts constructed at such a level of generality that they exhibit certain characteristics of traditional philosophical universals, while nonetheless carrying specific historical meanings. Such concepts are 'philosophical' to the extent that they are representations of universal elements of social practices, not just at the level of the content of these practices, but at the level of the modes of human social existence produced by their constitutive relations. That is, loosely speaking, they have the universality of the *categorial* in the Kantian sense, or the *existential* in Heidegger's terms. However, such concepts are nonetheless 'historical' in the sense that their universality has historical conditions of existence. That is to say, they are philosophical in an historically emergent and hence only retrospectively 'ontological' way. They are tensed in the future anterior: they aim to tell of the way things *will have been.* (All ontology is relative to the *prospectively retrospective*, speculative vision of the absolute present.) These concepts share a certain level of abstraction which specifies a certain dimension of social being.

One reason for suspicion of philosophy by other disciplines is the level of abstraction at which it constitutes its concepts. This frequently leads to either the postulation of an independent domain of the metaphysical, on the one hand, or a purely logical or methodological interpretation of these concepts, on the other. An anti-disciplinary approach to philosophical universality avoids these alternatives, but it does not thereby necessarily lower the level of abstraction, from the standpoint of the immediately concrete, which grounds all such talk of 'levels' of abstraction here. Rather, I shall argue, substantive cross-disciplinary generalities draw attention to the distinctive forms of abstraction which are constitutive of certain kinds of social relations, and hence also of certain forms of human subjectivity. This is their specifically cultural dimension: the cultural is the meaningful dimension of subject production.[41] That is to say, these cross-disciplinary abstractions are actual, qua abstractions: they are *abstract actualities* or *real abstractions*. As Marx put it in the *Grundrisse*: 'even the most abstract categories, despite their validity – precisely because of their abstractness – for all epochs, are nevertheless, in the specific character of this abstraction, themselves a product of historic relations and possess their full validity only for and within these relations.'[42] There is a whole theory of cross-disciplinary generality in this quotation.

Philosophers are those who, in Hegel's words, are 'at home in abstraction'.[43] Capitalist modernity is a social world constituted through abstraction to a hitherto unthinkable extent. It is in this conjunction that the 'absolute modernity' of an anti-disciplinary, and hence speculative and cross-disciplinary, philosophical practice resides. What I want to suggest is that what Marx wrote about the concept of labour is true also of general concepts in cultural theory, albeit in different ways. Examples of such concepts might be: *modernity, modernism, gender, sign, image, art, nation, colonialism, hybridity, sexuality, boredom* – a Borgesian list to be sure, but then the structure of an open totality is not logically hierarchical, but constellatory. Gender is no more a property of individuals than capital is a thing. Each is a social relation, constituted through, but by no means exhausted by, historically specific but socially diverse practices of recognition. (One could no more have masculinity without femininity than capital without labour.) Similarly, as we shall see in the next chapter, the ontologies of sign and image, as such, in their greatest generality, are constantly produced anew by the historical development of new technologies of image production. Philosophical interpretation and critique of such concepts can help refigure whole fields of cultural theory. Anti-philosophical philosophers and post-philosophical cultural theorists notwithstanding, it is that task to which the essays in this book aim to contribute.

2

SIGN AND IMAGE

The distance separating cultural studies in Britain and North America from the systematic, metaphysical and existential concerns of the post-Kantian tradition is epitomized by the ontological agnosticism, or methodologism, consequent upon the former's adoption of Saussurean linguistics as its model for a semiotic theory of culture. If the founding gesture of what was to become cultural studies was anthropological, it was the reception of structuralist semiotics from France in the early 1970s which simultaneously transformed the study of culture and established it as an intellectual field in its own right. However diverse its subsequent developments have been, cultural studies continues to be characterized, theoretically, by the focus on signifying practices which that reception inaugurated and the structuralist lineage or post-structuralist problematic which it set in place.[1] Just as any argument regarding the value to cultural theory of the conceptual resources of the systematic and metaphysical side of the post-Kantian tradition must pass through a critique of pragmatism, as its implicit (post-)philosophical self-understanding, so this critique needs to be extended to the conception of meaning through which cultural studies constitutes its objects. This provides an opportunity to develop some themes hinted at in the previous chapter – the importance but neglect of Peirce and the affinity of Peirce and Benjamin – and to introduce some new ones, such as the resonances between Benjamin's and the later Barthes' writings on photography.

More specifically, what follows suggests one particular way in which Benjamin's metaphysical conception of the image-spaces of historical experience offers an alternative to the post-Saussurean trajectory of cultural studies. A contextualizing sketch of the antinomy between semiotics and aesthetics (meaning and sensibility) that constitutes the field of cultural studies in its post-Saussurean form leads into a discussion of Peirce's semiotics, with its three-fold classification of types of sign, as the possible basis for a different approach. This raises the issue of the status of 'icon' and 'index' within a coded-based semiotics. This is pursued, in the first instance, through consideration of Eco's critique of Peirce's iconism and of contrasting attitudes to the semiotics of the photograph, respectively. Discussion of the indexicality of the photograph returns us to the question of the aesthetic dimension of meaning and thereby to the ontology of images. An account of the historical ontology of the photographic image provides the basis for a reformulation of the relationship between index-icality and iconicity in terms of technologies of reproduction, aimed at overcoming the antinomy of semiotic and aesthetic approaches. This is explored further via the metaphysical pragmatism of Peirce's theory of interpretants and its alignment with Benjamin's conception of historical experience.

Recent interest in Deleuze's writings represents a parallel movement to the Benjaminian approach to cultural form that is favoured here, in several respects. However, for all its immanent conceptual dynamism and open-ness to the new, the metaphysical naturalism of Deleuze's work places strict limits upon its applicability to cultural study, as a consequence of its dual refusal of a social ontology and a concept of history. A coda marks this thought.

Semiotics in cultural studies

Ever since Kant's transcendental critique of the intuitive grounds of Baumgarten's cognitivism severed the connection of aesthetics to semi-otics, in the aftermath of the birth of aesthetics as a philosophical discipline, at the end the eighteenth century, the two fields of enquiry have been fundamentally estranged. Today, it is no exaggeration to say that semi-otics and aesthetics form the torn, antinomic halves of an experience of cultural form between which contemporary debates about art and culture shuttle back and forth, in an anxious and decidedly non-dialectical oscil-lation. This split, internal to the comprehension of the image – a split between *signification* and *aesthesis*, meaning and sensibility – registers both the changing social function of images in capitalist societies conse-quent upon the declining of the power of the church (desacralization and commodified re-enchantment) and the development of new technologies of image-production. Yet these historical relations remain unreflected in the theoretical constitution of the two fields.

Kant's 'faculty' aesthetics divorced the theorization of the formal sensible qualities of the image from its representational function. Such is its materi-alism. Conversely, its counterpart, modern semiotics has come, increasingly, to treat this signifying function in abstraction from both its sensible and its existential qualities. This is apparent in the contrasting fortunes of the work of its two founding figures, C.S. Peirce and Ferdinand de Saussure.

Peirce's classification of types of sign famously included a distinction between three types of sign according to their relations to their objects –

21

icon, index, and symbol – which signify by virtue of *resemblance, causal connection*, and *convention, habit* or *acquired law*, respectively. It also accorded primacy to the icon as that type of sign which 'every assertion must contain', if only indirectly, via 'signs whose meaning is only explicable by icons'.[2] Since the 1950s, however, Peirce's icon has progressively fallen by the wayside of cultural and art theory, as the naturalism of the idea of non-conventional resemblance has been subjected to withering epistemological attack.[3] Effectively reduced by this attack to an authoritatively socially sanctioned visual form of the symbol, the icon was further marginalized by the rise to power in cultural theory during the 1960s of a Saussurean notion of the sign, in which the arbitrariness of the connection of the specifically *linguistic* signifier to the signified was extended to the sphere of signification in general, thereby obliterating any intrinsic representational dimension of visual form.

For such followers of Saussure, like the early Barthes, insofar as it signifies, the icon is rendered equivalent to a linguistic sign. Its visual or aural properties appear in their own right (that is, non-differentially) only as non-signifying aesthetic residues, which function within the process of the production of meaning as mere means or supports for arbitrary differential relations. The 'habit or acquired law' motivating Peirce's symbols are reduced to convention, and conventions are understood to be arbitrary relations.[4] Meanwhile, indexical relations fall outside the non-referential sway of Saussurean semiology altogether. In this way, as a form of 'translinguistics', Saussurean semiology produces and reproduces 'aesthetics' as its non-signifying other. Certain signs (in effect, signifiers) may *present* themselves as being directly related to certain referents, but this is an ideological function (a naturalization of a history of differences) which reveals them to be constituent parts of modern day myths.

This is not the place to tell the tangled tale of the role of semiotics in the transformation of cultural studies and allied disciplines, such as the transmogrification of art history into 'visual culture'. That history is significantly more complex, contradictory and nuanced than it is possible to convey here. Suffice to say: 1) that the power of the Saussurean paradigm derives from its combination of simplicity and generality, that is, from its reduction of signification to one kind, indifferent to the specificities of signifying materials; 2) that this generality and indifference had the effect of creating of a new trans- or anti-disciplinary object, the text;[5] 3) that this new object became the site for the articulation of semiotics to a particular psychoanalytical theory of the subject (Lacanianism);[6] 4) that this articulation of Saussurean or post-Saussurean semiotics and Lacanian metapsychology was, in turn, linked to various extensions of the model to the social, through its connection to Althusser's theory of ideology, Gramsci's concept of hegemony, and Foucault's notion of discourses;[7] 5) that subsequent accretions, such as a Derridean conception of difference or a deconstructive notion of performativity,[8] represent refinements rather than challenges to the evolution of the model.

In this process, the Saussurean origin of the model has been covered over by successive theoretical layerings and critical transpositions of its terms – in particular, an inversion of emphasis from *langue* to *parole* followed from closer consideration of the moment of enunciation. In this respect, it is Benveniste, more than Saussure, whose work in linguistics underlies the articulation of semiotic, psychoanalytical and Foucauldian paradigms that remains the mainstay of most Anglo-American cultural theorizing today.[9] Nonetheless, the trajectory established by Barthes' reception of Saussure remains in place: the aspiration to a semiotic account of culture on the basis of the generalization of a linguistic model.[10] As the model has developed, its constituent elements have all been transformed, in one way or another, by their reduction to this plane of signification, including their political aspects.

As a field, cultural studies distinguished itself from previous disciplinary approaches to contemporary culture by its concern for the role of meanings in the social organization of power. Initially, this concern took two main forms: an extension of the field of relevant objects and practices to totality (the democratic dimension of the anthropological move) and the deployment of the concept of ideology, to identify the political functions of the various objects and practices under consideration. In this respect, in its canonical Birmingham form, cultural studies developed out of interactions with sociology and Marxist historiography, as much as with semiotics. However, once what began as an uneven articulation of different disciplinary approaches to the social study of meaning acquired a unitary transdisciplinary theoretical medium – textuality – the question of power became internalized to this medium. As a result, it was transformed into the question of semiotic re-articulation: the capacity to disrupt and rebuild chains of signifiers, and through them to effect the 'positionalities' constitutive of social identities.

This textualization of politics has given rise to some fairly fruitless quasi-philosophical exchanges about whether there is anything 'outside' the text, in which outraged realists have traded misunderstandings with complacent textualists. But this is not a helpful formulation of the issue – and its spatial metaphorics are in any case ripe for deconstruction. There may not be any thing 'outside' the text, but then there isn't any 'thing' inside it either. (Derrida famously crossed out the 'is' in the slogan 'The Outside is the Inside'.) Epistemic attempts to resolve ontological disputes are doomed to failure. Rather, what is important about this phenomenon – the textualization of politics – is the way in which the ontological agnosticism of post-Saussurean semiotics *breaks down* once its framework is extended to politics. It cannot avoid some kind of ontologization of its semantic formalism – some recourse to discourse about being – if it is to become the medium of political thought. Yet its *direct* transposition into ontological mode, in discourse theory, is misplaced because unmediated.[11] The main candidate for mediation has been Lacan's semiotically reconstructed version of psychoanalytical theory. Psychoanalytical theory functions as a stand-in for ontology in cultural studies, grounding its ontologization of semiotics. Yet the semiotic and socio-sexual dogmatism of Lacanianism – its reduction of the complex relations between gender, sexuality, and sex difference to a universalized symbolic 'sexual difference', and its indifference to other forms of social difference – render it unsuitable for such a general philosophical role.[12] There is an urgent need for a more adequate general conception of the relations between semantic and existential-pragmatic forms. It is here that Peirce's work suggests itself as a basis for an alternative philosophical trajectory for semiotic cultural analysis.

Peirce's writings have an acknowledged place in the pre-history of cultural semiotics, but only a sporadic presence with little enduring resonance within it. It is striking that even on those occasions when the greater possibilities offered by his more differentiated and philosophically complex approach to meaning have been recognized – within cinema studies, art history and musicology – such recognition has either remained unexplored or been rapidly revoked. No sooner has the insight occurred than it is isolated and undone.[13] Indeed, it is notable that even the semiotician most influenced by Peirce, who believes that 'only from Peirce's point of view can many problems of contemporary text theories be satisfactorily solved', Umberto Eco, fundamentally reinterprets Peirce's distinction between icon, index and symbol reducing it to the terms of a non-referential theory of codes. At the same time, however, Eco embraces Peirce's theory of 'interpretants' as 'the missing link between semiosis and physical reality as practical action', the solution to the problems of 'the status of the meaning components' that the methodologism of Saussurean semiotics idealistically forecloses.[14] Eco thus simultaneously eliminates the referential dimension of Peirce's semiotics, whilst finding elsewhere within it the key to the mediation of semiotics with a pragmatist ontology. It is through a critical revision of this reading that the relevance of Peirce's work to cultural theory can be brought into view.

Peirce and Eco on the icon

Eco's appropriation of Peirce's semiotics has three main aspects: 1) a critique of the notion of 'types of sign' in the name of a more fluid classification of sign-functions and their various modes of production; 2) a critique of the unmediated naturalism of the referential semantics involved in Peirce's conceptions of icon and index; 3) an extension of Peirce's theory of interpretants from semantics to pragmatics, along with the 'surgical removal' of its residual mentalism. It is the relationship between

2) and 3) that is of interest here. Eco's first point is in any case consistent with Peirce's own sense that any particular signification will involve all three types of sign, in varying degrees. Peirce's (posthumously published) writings are fragmentary and frequently seemingly inconsistent. Eco's critical transformation of Peirce's position is in this respect often no more than the development of one interpretive possibility in preference to others.

Eco's *A Theory of Semiotics* (1976) sets out from a communicational definition of the object of semiotics ('semiotics studies all cultural processes as *processes of communication*'), while nonetheless insisting on the autonomy of systems of signification as semiotic constructs: 'A signification system ... has an abstract mode of existence independent of any possible communicative act it makes possible. On the contrary (except for stimulation processes) *every act of communication to or between human beings* – or any other intelligent biological or mechanical apparatus – *presupposes a signification system as its necessary condition*.'[15] Systems of signification, then, are transcendentally ideal, and as such may be studied formally, as conditions of possibility of communicative acts. As conditions of such acts, however, the relations of signification or signifying functions which make them up (the taking of something as 'standing for' something else) must always be capable of being a 'taking of something as standing for something else *for someone else*'.[16] As such, they depend upon social conventions associating particular sign-vehicles with particular contents, conventions which can themselves only be represented by other sign-vehicles. For all their transcendental-logical self-sufficiency, systems of signification are thus necessarily historically coded. Semiotics is, in large part, a theory of codes. A sign-function is 'the correlation between an expression and a content based on a conventionally established code (a system of correlational rules)'. Codes 'provide the rules that generate sign-functions'.[17]

Eco's critique of the referential naturalism of Peirce's conceptions of icons and indices as distinct types of sign follows directly from this approach. But it should not be assumed that conventions are arbitrary. Eco explicitly denies it: 'the notion of convention ... is not co-extensive with that of arbitrary link, but ... is co-extensive with that of *cultural* link.' However, in his view,

> [a] theory of codes may well disregard the difference between motivated and arbitrary signs, since it is only concerned with the fact that a convention exists which correlates a given expression to a given content, irrespective of the way in which the correlation is posited and accepted.[18]

A theory of codes posits a 'self-sufficient universe of content'.[19] This means that what Peirce describes as the discrete signifying structures of icons

and indices must actually be, in Eco's view, disguised forms of signification by convention, in so far as they signify at all.

The key to this account is the idea that 'iconism' – resemblance – is
not a relationship between an image and a referent (an actual physical
object) but a correlation between two images, both of which are coded:
a graphic sign-vehicle and a perceptual unit. The *illusion* of an unmediated
relation arises because 'in the iconic experience certain perceptual mechanisms function which are of the same type as the one involved in the
perception of an actual object'. Once we accept that all perceptual experience is based on certain recognition codes, however, 'the presumed
"naturalness" of resemblances dissolves itself into a network of cultural
stipulations that determine and direct ingenuous experience'. Indeed,
culturally, the *production* of resemblance works the other way around,
since it is largely on the basis of historically established graphic codes
that perceptual codes are learned. Similar points apply to diagrams (Peirce's
second kind of iconic sign): it is convention that 'establishes that certain
abstract relations [such as inclusion of a particular within a given set or
class] can be *expressed* by spatial relations'. On the other hand, the raw
fact of recognition which allows for the identification of a token sign-
vehicle as the token of a particular type is excluded by Eco from the
realm of semiotics, and treated as a postulate underlying its very possibility: 'The very notion of a sign and of its replicability (and thus of its
social nature) depends on postulating that such a recognition is possible.'
To consider such recognition iconic is to 'mistake for an icon what [is]
in fact a *constitutive condition* for the *impression* of iconism'. Iconism is
thus made up of 'hidden phenomena', some of which are not iconic, the
others of which 'can in no sense be viewed as semiotic' at all.[20]

I shall return to Eco's exclusion from semiotics of type-recognition in
sign-vehicles later, since it is integral to his attempt to sidestep or side-
line Peirce's realism. First, however, it is necessary to consider the index,
the third and most directly referential of Peirce's three types of sign. I
shall do so with respect to the photograph, for two reasons: first, because
it is the massive expansion in the social dissemination of photographic
imagery, in myriad functional contexts (documentation, souvenir, adver-
tising, journalism, surveillance, pornography), that accounts for the
importance of the index as a mode of signification of the real – the photograph was the dominant form of the image in the twentieth century, the
index, the dominant form of the sign; second, because the theory of
photography offers an alternative, historical and ontological approach to
indexicality, from the standpoint of which Peirce's semiotics appears in a
rather different light from Eco's interpretation.

The indexicality of the photograph

The photograph has long been considered a paradigmatic example of an indexical sign, or, as Barthes famously put it in his 1961 essay 'The Photographic Message', 'a message without a code'.[21] In Pierce's words, from the beginning of the last century:

> Photographs ... are very instructive because we know that they are in certain respects exactly like the objects they represent. But this resemblance is due to the photographs having been produced under such circumstances that they were physically forced to correspond point by point to nature. In that aspect then, they belong to the second class of signs, those by physical connection. ... The fact that ... [the photograph] is known to be the effect of the radiations from the object renders it an index and highly informative.[22]

Eco does not discuss photography in *A Theory of Semiotics*. He restricts his discussion of indices to the alleged indexicality of the verbal shifter 'I', arguing that it actually signifies by coding 'physical closeness' as its signified content.[23] However, there is no doubt that he would dismiss the indexical character of the photograph as a possible vehicle of signifying functions. In this respect, his conventionalism is more consistent than Barthes', since it would reject the very idea of a message without a code, in however restricted or dumb a form. Nonetheless, Barthes' early essay can usefully stand in for a conventionalist account, in comparison with Peirce, in order to examine the place of codes in photographic significa-tion. For Barthes' inconsistency here is less an intellectual flaw than a symptom of the limitations of the strict conventionalist approach.

Barthes acknowledges an indexical aspect to photographic signification, but he differs from Peirce about the relationship between this indexical aspect and the photograph's other, iconic and symbolic, dimensions. Crucially, for Peirce, the indexicality and iconicity of the photograph are mutually constitutive. It is not just that the physical connection between object and image in the photographic process *establishes* a relation of resemblance (analogy), but this relation (the iconic character of the image) is a condition of its interpretation as an index. For Peirce, there is no indexicality without resemblance. Effects only become indexes of their causes when also treated as icons. In this respect, on Eco's account, there will be no indexicality without a code (without a symbol), since all resem-blance is coded. However, from Peirce's standpoint, such conditionality is insufficient to *reduce* the signifying function of an index to its coding; as indeed it is also insufficient to *reduce* an icon to its conventional prop-erties. For just as there is more to indices than their own 'peculiar' iconicity,

so there is more to Peirce's notion of the icon than the relation of resemblance which defines its relation to its object. There is also what he calls
its '*firstness*'.

Peirce distinguished three ontological dimensions or aspects of the
process of signification, standing in a triadic relation:

> A *Sign*, or *Representamen*, is a First which stands in such a genuine
> triadic relation to a Second, called its *Object*, as to be capable
> of determining a Third, called its *Interpretant*, to assume the
> same triadic relation to its Object in which it stands itself to the same
> Object. The triadic relation is *genuine*, that is its three members are
> bound together by it in a way that does not consist in any complexus
> of dyadic relations. That is the reason the Interpretant, or Third,
> cannot stand in a dyadic relation to the Object, but must stand in
> such a relation to it as the Representamen itself does.[24]

And he associated Firstness with the icon. In his characteristically contorted
prose: 'An *Icon* is a Representamen whose Representative Quality is a
Firstness of it as a First. That is, a quality that it has *qua* thing renders
it fit to be a Representamen'.[25] Hence the primacy of the icon for Pierce
within semiotics as a whole. It is on the basis of this 'quality that it has
qua thing' that it enters into a relation to its object (acquires a Secondness)
interpreted as resemblance (Thirdness). That is, strictly speaking resemblance is the *third*, not primary, quality of an iconic sign. What are we
to make of this?

Eco disregards the ontological dimension of Firstness altogether, treating
it methodologically as a mere starting point for the reconstruction of
chains of Thirds/interpretants, each of which can act as a First, if placed
at the beginning of the chain. Yet for Peirce it is of crucial significance.
It is only because of a certain 'Firstness' – a certain 'quality that it has
qua thing' – that anything can become a sign, and hence that signification is possible. Furthermore, according to Peirce, 'its Representative
Quality is not necessarily dependent upon its ever actually determining
an Interpretant, nor even upon its actually having an Object.' Peirce called
this representative quality a 'hypoicon'. It is found in 'any material image
... in itself, without legend or label'.[26] Such is Peirce's semiotic naturalism, which makes his work so sympathetic to Deleuze. It is remarkably
similar to what André Bazin identified as the specific ontological quality
of the photographic image: 'the object itself ... freed from the conditions
of time and space that govern it ... an image that is a reality of nature'.
Bazin saw this quality as having been generalized by surrealism into a
new ontology, in which 'the logical distinction between what is imaginary and what is real tends to disappear. Every image is to be seen as
an object and every object as an image.'[27] Such is the pre-history of

Baudrillard's notion of the simulacrum. This peculiar ontological dimension of the image can be seen at work within even Barthes' restrictively Saussurean account of the photograph.

For the early Barthes, like Peirce, what is ontologically distinctive about the photograph is epistemologically secondary – namely, its indexicality or lack of a code – but the articulation between these elements is conceived in an altogether different way. Unsurprisingly for a coded account, what Barthes calls the 'analogical perfection' of the purely indexical 'message without a code', or 'photographic message proper', is treated as the mere ground or matter on which 'the "historical grammar" of iconographic connotation' is superimposed in the interpretation of any particular photograph. The purely analogical aspect communicates no representational content on its own. Despite Barthes' use of the term 'analogy', the photographic image is understood to contain no discrete iconic dimension, in Peirce's sense. More surprisingly, its indexical dimension *is* nonetheless seen to have a distinct semiological function: namely, to secure the 'denotative status' of the image, through which the connotations carried by the codes are naturalized. But this uncoded function operates only via the coded one (the symbolic dimension), which it serves retrospectively to ground as specifically 'photographic'.

This denotative status or naturalizing function of photographic indexicality derives from the same source as its iconic blindness: namely, its 'analogical perfection' – the fact that in itself the photographic message proper is *continuous*. It lacks semiological difference. Despite the formal (technical) acknowledgement of its resemblance to its field of objects (derived from the sciences of optics and chemistry), it is thus *unreadable* as a signifier for any particular set of objects, without the discontinuity introduced by a connotative symbolic supplement. Or to put it in another, more Kantian way, its 'object' is indeterminate. It signifies only 'the photographic' – meaning the purely or absolutely denotative – in general. The photographic aspect of the image denotes only denotation. The 'photographic message proper' is simply 'this is real'. Precisely *how* the photograph can convey this message, however, Barthes does not and, I would argue, *cannot* say, outside of the appeal to technical knowledge of the photographic process (the causal connection). Yet the deployment of such knowledge in any particular case presupposes the status of the photograph as a sign – that is, Peirce's Firstness. Without some such presupposition, there is no reason to approach the phenomenon semiotically in the first place. One way to read the functioning of Firstness here is *aesthetically*.

The aesthetic dimension

Saussurean and code-based semiotics, I have suggested, produce and reproduce 'aesthetics' as their non-signifying other. In this respect, they follow

29

the analytical philosophical tradition in viewing the world from a narrowly logical point of view.[28] The antipathy of the cultural studies and art theory of the 1970s and 1980s to anything connected to 'aesthetics' was well-nigh absolute. 'Aesthetics' appeared there pretty much as a synonym for 'connoisseurship': an anti-intellectual form of cultural élitism, whose claims to universality are based on little more than inherited authority, shrouded by the mystical veil of intuitive judgement. However, this critical description applies only to a modified Humean aestheticism which has borrowed the notion of indeterminate judgement from the Kantian tradition, and analytically misconstrued it.[29] From this point of view, as Urmson put it in his encyclopaedia entry on 'aesthetics' from 1960, 'aesthetics, more than any other branch of philosophy seems doomed either to pretentious vagueness or to an extreme poverty which makes it a poor step-sister to other main fields of philosophical enquiry'.[30] From the point of view of analytical logic, indeterminate judgement appears as 'pretentious vagueness' or 'extreme poverty of content'. Hence the inherent awkwardness of 'analytical aesthetics': too analytical and too aesthetic, by turns, for its own philosophical conscience to bear. Yet this negative logical judgement of aesthetics itself derives from an impoverished range of logical forms. For on its Kantian construal, aesthetic judgement is not merely 'indeterminate' – lacking in conceptual determinacy – but 'reflective'. It is not the mere negative of determinate judgement, but a logically distinct type of judgement. Furthermore, Kant's account of aesthetic judgement subtlely combines an 'inward' and an 'outward' reference for 'aesthetic'. It is this duality of reference or doubling of 'aesthetic' that provides it with its broader, metaphysical and existential significance. The Kantian conception of aesthetic judgement opens up the possibility of a more complex account of the relationship between the *aesthetic*, the *semantic* and the *ontological* dimensions of the photographic image.

Kant's 'Critique of Aesthetic Judgement' (1790) is a study in the cognitive ambiguity of the aesthetic. On the one hand, in its core 'outward' sense, 'aesthetic' refers to the independent functioning of the faculty of sensibility (sensible intuition of space and time), the transcendental doctrine of which is proffered as the first part of the Transcendental Doctrine of Elements in the *Critique of Pure Reason*. Here, aesthetic is *opposed to* and *excludes* the understanding, which is the seat of concepts, conceived as representations of forms of judgement. But aesthetic is nonetheless an indispensable element of knowledge. On the other hand, insofar as 'aesthetic' is also the name for a particular kind of judgement – 'non-conceptual' or indeterminate judgements of the beautiful and the sublime – it refers 'inwards' to a relation of reflection between the faculty of sensibility and those of the understanding and reason, respectively. Here, 'aesthetic' *includes* reference to the two other cognitive faculties. Kant's notorious anti-cognitivism in aesthetics is in this regard a consequence of the limitations of his conception of cognition, rather than of any kind of purism of the senses. Most fundamentally, aesthetic judgement is concerned with the feeling of pleasure occasioned by the experience of the harmony/dissonance of the faculties and hence with the unity/disunity of subjectivity itself. In this respect, it marks a movement towards an experience of totality: a metaphysics of subjectivity as the relational totality of cognitive faculties.[31]

Furthermore, in its extension of aesthetic beyond sensibility to the relations between the faculties, Kant's notion of aesthetic judgement links aesthetic experience to *meaning* and *signification*. Aesthetic experience is a conceptually indeterminate experience of meaning. More precisely, as reflective judgement, it is an experience of the endless *process* of signification as the production and immanent destruction of signifiers or sign-vehicles in the interpretive apprehension of material form.[32] Kant lacked a theory of meaning, but he came close to a notion of aesthetic signification in his formulation of 'aesthetic ideas': 'unexpoundable presentations of the imagination (in free play) . . . intuition[s] (of the imagination) for which . . . adequate concept[s] can never be found'. Aesthetic experience, on this model, 'compares the given presentation in the subject with the entire presentational power, of which the mind becomes conscious when it feels its own state', that is to say, with 'cognition in general'. 'When this happens, the cognitive powers brought into play by the presentation are in free play, because no determinate concept restricts them to a particular rule of cognition.'[33] Hermeneutically speaking, the comprehension of aesthetic ideas is thus an infinite task, determinacy of meaning is endlessly deferred (hence the affinity with deconstruction), despite the fact that a judgement is made. Indeed, apprehension of the infinity or freedom of play between the powers is the very basis of the judgement.

Aesthetic judgements are thus *not* judgements of meaning, in any conventional sense (such as settling upon an interpretation), but they do nonetheless require an interpretative process of meaning-seeking as their experiential ground. However, this process is defined, not by the relations between signifiers (it is not the infinite semiosis of an enunciatory semantics), but by a constant fracturing of their *formation*. As Menke puts it: 'every effort to answer the question as to what an aesthetic object might mean is confronted by the even more basic question of what, if anything, in this object signifies (i.e. conveys meaning or is significant)'.[34] It is this fundamental indeterminacy regarding which aspects of the object are significant – the fact that there is 'no particular rule of cognition' – that underlies and sustains the indeterminacy of any particular interpretation. The indeterminacy of the aesthetic signification is more fundamental than the indeterminacy of meaning revealed by the deconstruction of Saussurean semiotics. In this respect, it is confusing of Menke to refer to 'aesthetic signifiers', when, as he himself explains, it is the 'vacillation' or 'trembling'

31

of signifers between the poles of materiality and meaning which is at stake.[35] The aesthetic is not a type of signifier, or even a mode of signification, strictly speaking, but a type or aspect of the *experience* of meaning. In articulating a special kind of experience of meaning, across the gap between materiality and meaning, it represents a critique of the concept of the signifier itself.

Eco's attempt to incorporate aesthetics into semiotics as a special use of the elements of a code – *invention* or *code-changing* – misses this fundamental point, although his account of the dependence of the 'aesthetic text' upon a manipulation of expression designed to release a reassessment of content implicitly relies upon it. On this account, an aesthetic text is one in which 'the matter of the sign-vehicle becomes an aspect of the expression-form', such that every 'free variation' of the sign-vehicle acquires a formal value. Following Jakobson's analysis of the poetic function, its message thereby becomes 'ambiguous' and 'self-focusing' since its signifying features violate the established rules of its codes. However, despite the fact that this account *appears* to be about matter ('in the aesthetic sign-vehicle matter . . . has been rendered semiotically interesting') it is actually about a *lower level* of coding, or a finer segmentation of the continuum of the matter of the sign-vehicle. This becomes apparent when Eco appeals to 'an *empirical limit* beyond which this material consistency, even though segmented to its utmost, can only be viewed . . . as a *cluster* of unpredictable hypoforms'. 'Beyond this limit', he continues, 'there may still be perceptive and emotional effects but there are no more significations. Once it has moved beyond this threshold the work of art seems to *stimulate reactions* but not to *communicate contents*.'[36]

Eco emphasizes the word 'cluster', but the word 'unpredictable' is equally important. Violations of the rules that fail to follow rules for the violation of rules are semiotically unintelligible: not 'significations', but mere 'reactions'. The specifically aesthetic dimension is systematically excluded here, in the guise of an 'empirical limit' to its inclusion. Unable to account for the singularity characteristic of the logical form of aesthetic judgements, appeal is made to a base layer of 'reactions', beyond meaning. Yet, if anything, the concept of reaction suggests a *law-governed* response, of stricter universality than the rules of a code. Meanwhile, the intelligibility of the whole account (the semiotic reduction of the aesthetic) depends upon understanding this region, beyond the limit, as simultaneously irreducible and potentially reducible matter. This contradiction can only be avoided if one accepts the 'unpredictability of hypoforms', and hence an indeterminacy of sign-function and sign-vehicle, played out in an experimental process of interpretation, as the defining characteristic of the aesthetic itself.

Within this semiotic reconstruction of Kantian aesthetics, 'aesthetic' signifies once again at two levels, corresponding to the two – 'outward' and 'inward' – uses by Kant: 1) as the *other* of semiotic, pure sensibility/ materiality, fracturing all attempts to select a determinate set of signifiers from the matter of the sign-vehicle; 2) as the double movement of the construction and destruction of meaning, the dynamic relation between semiosis and materiality.

Barthes' notion of the 'continuity' of the photograph grasps the first of these two senses of 'aesthetic' as lack of semiological difference: the continuum that must be segmented into units of expression, inserted into sign-functions, in order to signify. However, he fails to reflect sufficiently either upon its dialectical relation to semiosis or upon its ontological basis – the peculiar mode of its participation in the real. A photograph does not just 'denote' denotation, via the difference between its analogical continuity and the discontinuity of its codes – the 'matter' of *all* sign-vehicles is continuous, by definition – it instantiates an *aesthetically specific relation* between the brute continuity of matter and the semiotic discontinuities which it grounds. Furthermore, this relation carries with it a specific ontological charge.

On Kant's model, the pleasure of aesthetic reflection is a register of the unity or affinity of the cognitive powers within the subject. But it requires a certain kind of presentation for its occasion. Kant himself was relatively indifferent to the immanent characteristics of such presentations, since it was the relations between the powers that they occasion which concerned him. He thus characterized them wholly subjectively, in terms of their affects. Nonetheless, as the first sense of 'aesthetic' indicates, this affinity between the cognitive powers is at the same time an affinity between the object, as it appears within sensibility, and understanding or reason. That is to say, the aesthetic object (an object in its aesthetic aspect) must be such as to sustain interpretation.[37] 'Aesthetic', we might say, marks an intelligibility inherent within materiality, a potential interpretability. What I want to suggest is that this is what Peirce called 'Firstness': that 'quality that [an icon] has *qua* thing [which] renders it fit to be a representamen' or sign. The supposedly 'unreadable' continuity of analogical perfection constituted by the indexicality of the photographic process imparts to the photograph a specific Firstness, its own specific form of aesthetic totality. The existential-ontological charge of the photograph derives from the way in which this aesthetic quality carries its specific mode of indexical signification. The analytical category into which the photograph falls by virtue of this connection is neither the Saussurean 'sign' nor the Kantian 'aesthetic', but the theological *image*.

The historical ontology of the photographic image

This notion of the image, or *ikon* in the traditional sense, long pre-dates its modern semiotic interpretation, in which an epistemological conception of resemblance as copy predominates. It is the virtue of this older notion of the image that it combines the aesthetic, spatio-temporal concretion of an object of sight with the element of ideality inherent in ideas. This has always been its essential mediating function, from its understanding in ancient rhetoric as the graphic manifestation of an idea (registered in the etymological connection of *eidos*/idea to *eidelon*/image) – without which, according to Aristotle, 'the soul never thinks'[38] – to the modernist, surrealist and dialectical images of Pound, Carlos Williams, and Benjamin. Whether it be understood objectivistically, as in the Judeo-Christian tradition, as 'the essential reality of a thing', or subjectivistically, as in the proto-Romantic productive imagination and ambiguous concept-image of Kant's schematism, an image has always been a visual presentation of reality, at once sensuously particular and ideal.[39]

In combining aesthetic particularity with ideality in this way, relative to the infinite particularity of sensible intuition, on the one hand, and the logical determinacy of a concept which abstracts from all particularity, on the other, the notion of the image shares something with the notion of form to be found in Kant's conception of a pure, reflective judgement of taste – the latter notion being increasingly constitutive of 'aesthetic' in its restrictive modern sense as the domain of the beautiful and the ugly, the domain of taste. However, for all its sensuousness, this notion of form remains more abstract than the image since it is essentially subjective and excludes all reference to a representational function; hence its suitability to the late, optically reductive version of Greenberg's formalist modernism. In its inherent representational function, the notion of the image exceeds the domain of the Kantian aesthetic, without, however, sacrificing presence to meaning in the manner of Saussurean or code-based semiotics. In particular, its theological history of ontological surrogacy, as carrier of the divine,[40] offers a conceptual model for the unification of iconicity with indexicality.

Just as indices signify *qua* indices only via their iconicity (that Firstness which makes them recognizable as a sign), so the theological image or icon signifies *qua* icon (as a resemblance) only via its participation in, or quality of being the product/index of, the thing it represents (the divine). It is this broader, ontological sense of resemblance as the sharing of properties between a thing and its product that is at work in Peirce's notion of the icon. On this model, indexicality and iconicity are mutually dependent sign-functions. However, in the theological instance, the indexicality of the icon is unobservable, since the purported causal relation is supernatural: there is no 'physical connection'. It is an observable, natural-scientific version of this form of signification – which has earlier been given secular literary form in Coleridge's 'symbol' – that is found, paradigmatically, in the photograph. The invention of photography brought into existence a new ontological form, naturalizing the theological structure of the image. Photography is a theological technology: the secular paradigm for the participation of meaning in the real. It is this 'magical' aspect of photographic naturalism that stands at the centre of an ontological tradition of writing about photography which runs from Kracauer, through Benjamin and Bazin, to Barthes' final book, *Camera Lucida*.

The ontological properties of the photographic image follow from its specific indexicality: that is, the optical and chemical processes whereby the light reflected by objects, which allows us to perceive them, is imprinted directly onto light-sensitive surfaces, modelling the field of visual perception in a mechanical mimesis. These properties are: 1) participation of the photograph in the *being* of its referent; and hence 2) a direct, unmediated presence of the past within the present, or an *immobilization of time*. As Bazin put it: 'the image ... shares, by virtue of the very process of its becoming, the being of the model of which it is the reproduction: it *is* the model'; 'photography ... embalms time, rescuing it ... from its proper corruption.'[41] Or Barthes: 'The photograph is literally an emanation of the referent ... light, though impalpable, is here a carnal medium, a skin I share with anyone who has been photographed'; 'In the Photograph, Time's immobilization assumes ... an excessive, monstrous mode: Time is engorged.'[42]

Corresponding to these ontological properties are certain distinctive representational properties of the image and certain distinctive existential modes associated with photography as a cultural form. In the first case, there is the photograph's objectivism or *indifference* to the elements of its visual field, allied to its *contingency*. In the second, there is its special relationship to *death*, *memory* and *possibility*. These features are linked. However, the historical significance of this network of relations is the subject of interpretive dispute. Kracauer, for example, reads the objectivism of the photographic archive Romantically, within the problematic of an 'alienation from meaning', as a 'warehousing' or 'general inventory' of the disintegrated elements of nature – cultural equivalent to the role of nature within the capitalist mode of production. As such, the photograph stands in opposition to memory, art, history and even pastness itself.

> Photography grasps what is given as a spatial (or temporal) continuum; memory images retain what is given only in so far as it has significance ... from the perspective of memory, photography appears as jumble that consists partly of garbage.
>
> ... in the artwork the meaning of the object takes on spatial appearance, whereas in photography the spatial appearance is its meaning.
>
> In inverse proportion to photographs, memory images enlarge themselves into monograms of remembered life. The photograph is the sediment which has settled from the monogram, and from

year to year its semiotic value decreases. The truth content of the original is left behind in its history; the photograph captures only the residuum that history has discharged ... the spatial configuration of a moment ... the spatial continuum ... dominates the spatial appearance of the perceived object; the resemblance between the image and the object effaces the contours of the object's 'history'.

[Viewers] think they glimpse a moment of time past, a time that passes without return ... photographs by their sheer accumulation attempt to banish ... the recollection of death, which is part and parcel of every memory image.

Kracauer associated this 'disorder of the detritus' of nature in photography with 'the suspension of every habitual relationship among the elements of nature'. In contrast, he put his hopes in 'the game that film plays with the pieces of disjointed nature' to construct images of an alternative 'organization of things'.[43]

There can be few more powerful critiques of photography as a cultural form. However, it relies in large part upon a backward-looking contrast with positive metaphysical concepts of nature, memory, art and history which have lost their social basis, or at the least, need rethinking under conditions of modernity. If they are to retain a critical purchase, they will have to be recovered, transformed, from reflection on the structures of contemporary practices – as indeed Kracauer attempted, to some extent, elsewhere in his writings. Benjamin and the late Barthes undertook a similar task with regard to the photograph itself. They did not reject Kracauer's analysis, so much as complement it, dialectically, by focusing upon other, contrasting aspects of the experience of the photograph.

In 'Rhetoric of the Image' (1964), Barthes had already identified the 'truly unprecedented' type of consciousness associated with the 'anthropological revolution' of the photograph, as stemming from 'an illogical conjunction between the *here-now* and the *there-then*'. But he had classified its relation to the present as 'unreal', arguing that 'the photograph ... is in no way a *presence*'.[44] In *Camera Lucida*, on the other hand, the photograph appears as 'a certificate of presence', 'authentication itself'. 'To ask whether a photograph is analogical or coded is not a good means of analysis', Barthes now argues, '[t]he important thing is that the photograph possesses an evidential force, and that its testimony bears not on the object but on time.' What is authenticated here is contingency itself. Photography offers an immobilized experience of contingency which is of profound metaphysical relevance and existential force: 'the unheard-of identification of reality (*'that-has-been'*) with truth (*'there-she-is!'*) ... that crazy point where affect (love, compassion, grief, enthusiasm, desire) is a guarantee of Being.'[45]

The key to this new reading is the way in which the indifference of the photographic continuum to the elements within its field allows it to capture some unintended or unmarked particularity, that affects the viewer so intensely as to break through the photograph's representational shield (Kracauer's 'wall of likeness') and bear witness to the sheer existence of the referent itself. Barthes calls this detail the '*punctum*': 'that accident that pricks me (but also bruises me, is poignant to me).' It is the pure contingency of the photograph, registered in the *punctum* by way of 'a kind of amorous preference', that gives it, for Barthes, its metonymic historical significance: 'Photography has the same relation to History that the biographeme has to biography.' And this, precisely because of its difference from memory (Barthes agrees with Kracauer about that):

> The Photograph does not call up the past (nothing Proustean in a photograph). The effect it produces on me is not to restore what has been abolished (by time, by distance) but to attest that what I see has indeed existed.

'However lightning-like it may be', the metonymic role of the *punctum* gives it 'a power of expansion' (much like Kracauer's memory image) which connects it to historical being; whereas the '*studium*', its culturally coded counterpart or representational content, restricts it to its chronological historical context. If, as Kracauer put it, in a photograph 'a person's history is buried as if under a layer of snow', the *punctum* burns through the snow at a precise but contingent point, turning the photograph into something not unlike Kracauer's 'last [memory] image' which 'preserves the unforgettable ... elements that touch on what has been recognized to be true'. There is a dialectic here between the 'anything whatever' of photography's objective indifference (which is also its democratic aspect, the documentation of the everyday as the public face of the private) and the tiny 'something' which overwhelms the viewer, the 'detonation' of the 'intense immobility' of a detail.[46]

The similarity to certain of Benjamin's most characteristic formulations is striking. Barthes' 'amorous preference', 'sovereign contingency', the detail, the 'strange stasis of arrest', the triggering of an 'explosion', the 'unexpected flash', the 'wakening of intractable reality', every photograph the 'catastrophe' of a future death, 'a *magic*, not an art'[47] – all find more or less precise correspondents in Benjamin's 'A Small History of Photography' (1931) or in the methodological writings on the photographic quality of a political historiography from the late 1930s.[48] (Conversely, Kracauer had modelled his critique of photography on the critique of historicism, by mapping the former's spatial onto the latter's temporal 'continuum'.) However, there are also important differences, with broader implications for the discussion of indexicality and iconicity: differences concerning death and futurity,

37

singularity and reproduction. They hinge on the precise character of the photograph's representation of time.

Time and reproducibility

Towards the end of *Camera Lucida*, in formalizing the opposition of the metaphysical-existential experience of the *punctum* to the semiological character of the *studium*'s field of cultural interest, Barthes suddenly deepens his analysis by introducing what calls 'another *punctum* (another "stigmatum")': 'This new *punctum*, which is no longer of form [the detail] but of intensity, is Time, the lacerating emphasis of the *noeme* ("*that-has-been*"), its pure representation.' However, this is not actually a new *punctum,* as Barthes supposes, so much as a summary of the metaphysical affect of the *punctum per se.* Barthes finds it in the photograph of a young man (Lewis Payne, 1865) condemned to death. He calls this *punctum*: 'he is going to die'. But this is actually the *studium*: the condemned man waiting to be hanged. It could have been the caption if the photograph has appeared in an illustrated newspaper. Rather, it is what Barthes *reads into* what he is erroneously calling the punctum here which is important (for me, the *punctum* is the young man's eyes):

> *This will be* and *this has been* ... an anterior future of which death is the stake. By giving me the absolute past of the pose (aorist), the photograph tells me death in the future. What *pricks* me is the discovery of this equivalence. ... Whether or not the subject is already dead, every photograph is this catastrophe.

It is in the individualizing address of this message (a message without a code?) that Barthes finds the melancholic existential meaning of photography.

> It is because each photograph always contains this imperious sign of my future death that each one, however attached it seems to be to the excited world of the living, challenges each of us, one by one, outside of any generality (but not outside of any transcendence ... there is always a defeat of Time ... *that* is dead and *that* is going to die ... how alive they are! They have their whole lives before them; but also they are dead (today), they are then *already* dead (yesterday). At the limit, there is no need to represent a body in order for me to experience this vertigo of time defeated.[49]

How different both the depressed tone and philosophical consequences of this inverted Heideggerianism are (which finds mortality in the photographic defeat of time, rather than finding time itself, as temporalization, in mortality) from Benjamin's structurally similar analysis of

an irresistible urge to search ... [a photograph] for the tiny spark
of contingency, of the Here and Now, with which reality has so
to speak seared the subject, to find the inconspicuous spot where
in the immediacy of that long-forgotten moment the future subsists
so eloquently that we, looking back, may rediscover it.[50]

For Barthes, the inevitability of death, the defeat of time; for Benjamin,
the rediscovery of the future. For Barthes, the future as future death; for
Benjamin, futurity, possibility and hence politics.[51]

The difference derives from Barthes' undialectical opposition of the
punctum and the *studium* – in particular, his separation of the *punctum*
from knowledge – in contrast to Benjamin's elaboration of the connections between photographic technology, knowledge, and experience. Thus,
Barthes distinguishes the *punctum*, in principle, from photographic 'shock':
the revelation of 'what was so well hidden that the actor himself was
unaware or unconscious of it'.[52] Benjamin, on the contrary, famously char-
acterizes photography in terms of its discovery of an 'optical unconscious',
linking its technologically-based revelation of 'the physiognomic aspects
of visual worlds which dwell in the smallest things' (faster lenses, enlarge-
ment) to its rediscovery of the future. Furthermore, he extended this
modernist problematic of technology, knowledge and futurity into the
historical and political framework of 'the emancipation of object from
aura' and the social function of mechanical reproduction.[53]

Camera Lucida was Barthes' 'protestation of singularity' against all
reductive systems. His attempt to extend his individuality into a 'science
of the subject' that would attain to 'a generality which neither reduces
nor crushes me', an 'impossible science of the unique being'[54] – aesthetics,
perhaps. In this respect, it is the sister text to *Roland Barthes* (another
book of photographs), where it is written of structuralism that in it 'the
system prevails over the very being of objects'. In turning to the photograph as that object whose being offers the greatest possibility for such
a 'scientific' experience of singularity, Barthes turned against the dual
reduction of the image to the sign and the imaginary (image = sign +
imaginary) which had characterized his previous work, including the auto-
biography. But he made singularity into a fetish.[55] He refused to draw
theoretical implications from his analysis and, crucially, he ignored the
reproducibility of the photographic image: the fact that negative-based
photographic prints are multiples and can make multiples of any image
so reproduced. What I want to suggest is that 'the generality which neither
reduces nor crushes' is the *generality of reproduction*. Reproducibility is
the key to the relationship between iconicity and indexicality, singularity
and generality of meaning. For 'reproducibility' (replicability) is at once
a concept of semiotics and a socio-historically specific set of techniques.

The specificity of the photograph lies in the fact that it derives an 'evidential force' from the temporal singularity of its referent in such a way that it is, nonetheless, infinitely reproducible – even if never actually further reproduced.[56] As such, it is paradigmatic of the relationship between meaning and signification (in the specific semiotic sense) in the experience of images more generally. For there is an aesthetic dimension to the experience of meaning – Firstness, a quality that the image has *qua* thing – that exceeds its semiotic content and opens it up to indexical interpretation, opening it out onto the field of history. All objects are indices of their historical time. The irreducibly aesthetic dimension to the signifying function of the photographic image (the 'all-over' continuity of its surface) is the carrier of a specifically historical meaning. As Benjamin saw, it is their 'historic indexicality' that 'differentiates images from the "essences" of phenomenology'.[57] What unites the two dimensions of meaning here (aesthetic/indexical and conventional/symbolic) is the reproducibility of the pictorial image. As Adorno put it:

> There is an obvious qualitative leap between the hand that draws an animal on the wall of a cave and the camera that makes it possible for the same image to appear simultaneously at innumerable places. But the objectivation of the drawing vis-à-vis what is unmediately seen already contains the potential of the technical procedure that effects the separation of what is seen from the subjective act of seeing. Each work, insofar as it is intended for many, is already its own reproduction.[58]

Each work, insofar as it is intended for many, is already its own reproduction. Reproducibility is the ground of iconicity. Type-recognition in sign-vehicles is the subjective correlate of reproducibility.[59] Different techniques of reproduction (forms of indexicality) produce different (aesthetically specific) forms of iconicity. The image is what is visually reproducible, in this broad sense: a visual sign, conventional, but never merely conventional: iconic.

What the photograph taught Benjamin about the image is that the key to the icon is not 'resemblance' in some representational sense, but reproducibility: an analogical relation produced by an indexical connection, *a 'rule of construction' (Peirce) derived from a law of production.* Benjamin replaced the simple theological unity of the image's participation in the divine with the multiform, materially diverse, series of concrete unities of indexicality and iconicity made up by the history of technical reproduction. (This is the metaphorical moment in Benjamin's thought: displacement of the theological structure of the image into the history of technologies of image-production.) This is the conceptual importance of Benjamin's writings on the image: they ground the semiotic 'replicability' of the pictorial image (condition of its signifying function) in its means of reproduction.

The focus on technologies of reproduction functions here to unite several different levels of analysis – sense perception, signification, social use, and historical meaning – within the terms of a philosophical concept of experience. In particular, it draws attention to the technological organization (and reorganization) of experience through images.[60] As such, it is a central concept of cultural politics. For cultural politics is not just about the *coding* of subject-production, it is also about the formation of subjects as practical, embodied, technologically organized structures of experience. In themselves, such structures are politically ambiguous, the possible ground of radically different social practices. It is precisely because of this, however, that political thinking needs to take them into account. This returns us to the relationship of semiotics to ontology (existential pragmatics) and the critical historical function of a speculative concept of truth.

Meaning and historical experience

Eco reinterpreted Peirce's notions of icon and index within the terms of a non-referential theory of codes, but he nonetheless retained elements of Peirce's pragmatism in two ways: 1) in his use of Peirce's theory of inference to account for the way in which codes are established for indices; 2) in his adoption of Peirce's understanding of habit as 'the final logical interpretant' of an intellectual sign. In each case, semiotics appears as part of a broader theory of experience. At the same time, however, the concept of experience is naturalized in such a way as to abstract from its cultural-historical forms and dynamics.

Eco explains the process by which imprints (a particularly iconic type of index, including the photograph) come to be conventionally coded as follows:

> Imprints (like any other recognition procedure) are *conventionally* coded, but the code is not established by an arbitrary social decision but is instead motivated by *previous experiences*; the correlation between a given form and given content has been mediated by a series of mentions, inferences based on uncoded circumstances, meta-semiotic statements. Since the experience of an event was constantly associated with a given imprinted form, the correlation, first *proposed* as the result of an inference, was then *posited*.[61]

The formalism of Eco's conventionalism is clear. What makes a correlation 'conventional' (and thus a possible sign-function) is the mere fact of its 'positing' as a rule. The general claim that 'codes provide the rules that generate sign-functions'[62] thus turns out to be misleading. Rather, in the case of indices, the rules that generate sign-functions are 'provided by' (proposed as the inferential results of) experience, including, most importantly, the experience of the experimental sciences. Codes merely codify them, that is, posit them as the ground of possible sign-functions, or present them as semiotic material. Lurking beneath the conventionalism of Eco's semiotics here is a *mediated naturalism*. This naturalism is to be found in Peirce's theory of interpretants in the pragmatic concept of habit. After all, what would lead to the positing of the inferential result of a particular body of experience as the ground of a sign-function, except some particular communicative *use*? It may formally be the case that

> [a] theory of codes may well disregard the difference between motivated and arbitrary signs, since it is only concerned with the fact that a convention exists which correlates a given expression to a given content, irrespective of the way in which the correlation is posited and accepted.[63]

But a general semiotics cannot so disregard it. Semiotics exceeds the theory of codes. For the processes of communication which are its object are grounded in inferential structures of experience that impart to the vehicles of different types of sign-function different existential-ontological modes. The differences between such modes are an integral part of the experience of meaning, but they cannot be grasped at the level of codes, as the account of the photograph, above, has shown. Existential modalities of meaning are one of the things at stake in the movement within Peirce's theory of interpretants from semantics to pragmatics.

Peirce's theory of interpretants is about the 'thirdness' or interpretive dimension of the signifying process: the way in which the relationship between a sign and its object is manifest as meaning. (A sign is 'something which stands *to somebody* for something in some respect or capacity'.) Peirce held that the 'first logical interpretant' was an idea produced in the mind of the interpreter. However, he did not believe that interpretants need be of 'a mental mode of being'. Alongside logical interpretants there are 'emotional' and 'energetic' ones too. (Emotional interpretants are feelings; energetic interpretants are acts of muscular or mental effort.) Indeed, Peirce recognized that the ultimate logical interpretant of a sign could *never* be a mental representation, since 'every thought is a sign' requiring its own interpretant, and so on *ad infinitum*, in 'an endless series of representations' or unlimited semiosis – a scenario praised by Derrida for having gone 'very far in the direction that I have called the de-construction of the transcendental signified'.[64] The idea of an ultimate logical interpretant (determination of conceptual meaning) thus requires an interpretant with sufficient generality to be deemed 'logical' but which is not a mental representation (which would always be another sign requiring interpretants of its own). However, if there is such a thing, will it not be at odds with the very idea of infinite semiosis (deferral of meaning) that aligns the theory of interpretants with deconstructive semiotics (grammatology)? On the other hand, if there is no such thing, in what sense could there ever be communicable 'meaning' at all?

A clue to the solution of this dilemma is to be found in the fact that, unlike Derrida, for the metaphysical Peirce, the endless series of mental logical interpretants 'may be conceived to have an absolute object as its limit'.[65] Otherwise one would have to give up the idea of a sign as 'something which stands to somebody *for something* in some respect or capacity'. Meaning is distinct from but parasitic upon the idea of reference, which functions at its limit. For all its infinite semiosis, Eco's 'self-sufficient universe of content' is thus, for Peirce, circumscribed on its outside by an absolute object. The final logical interpretant of any particular sign – should there be one – will establish a relation of the subject to this absolute object. And for Peirce there *are* final logical interpretants of intellectual signs (only 'intellectual' signs have logical interpretants): namely, *habits*.

> It can be proved that the only mental effect that can be so produced [as an interpretant] and that is not a sign [which would lead to an infinite regress] but is of a general application is a *habit-change*; meaning by a habit-change a modification of a person's tendencies towards action, resulting from previous experiences or from previous exertions of ... will or acts, or from a complexus of both kinds.

Habit is the 'essence' of the logical interpretant. 'The real and living logical conclusion [of the "inner worldly experimentation" that is interpretive activity] *is* that habit.' Even if habit is considered a sign, it is 'not a sign in that way in which that sign of which it is the logical interpretant is a sign.' For it stands midway between an intellectual sign and an action:

> The habit conjoined with the motive and the conditions has the action for its energetic interpretant; but action cannot be a logical interpretant because it lacks generality. ... But how otherwise can a habit be described than by a description of the kind of action to which it gives rise, with the specification of the conditions and of the motive?[66]

The final *logical* interpretant of a sign is a habit, but this is further interpreted, at any particular time, energetically, in an act – and no doubt also emotionally, in a feeling about or corresponding to the habit.

Eco takes this to mean that it is *action* which 'ends the game of semiosis': 'an energetic interpretant does not need to be interpreted; rather, it produces (I guess, by further repetitions) a change of habit.'[67] This is intuitively plausible and satisfyingly decisive, but badly wrong – in a way that mirrors the decisionism of deconstructive ethics. For something that is not itself a logical interpretant cannot, in principle, end the 'endless series of mental representations' which are logical interpretants (outside of death). On Peirce's account, an energetic interpretant 'never can be the meaning of an intellectual concept, since it is a single act, [while] such a concept is of a general nature'. If it could, the problem of determinacy of meaning would never have arisen in the first place. Moreover, Peirce explicitly rejects the model of habit as grounded in repetitive action, rather than mental effort.[68] Energetic interpretants may be 'singular' *qua* acts, but they are nonetheless themselves logically interpretable. As de Lauretis puts it,

> If the chain of meaning comes to a halt, however temporarily, it is by anchoring itself to somebody, some body, an individual subject. . . . the notion of habit as 'energetic attitude', a somatic disposition at once abstract and concrete, the crystallized form of past muscular/mental effort, is powerfully suggestive of a subject touched by the practice of signs, a subject physically implicated or bodily engaged in the production of meaning, representation and self-representation . . . *The individual's habit as a semiotic production is both the result and the condition of the social production of meaning.*[69]

Eco regresses to a behavioural reduction of habit in order to avoid the question of the subject. In doing so, he negates the *conjectural* character of logical interpretants which renders the notion of 'final' logical interpretants consistent with both the infinite semiosis of mental representations and Peirce's realism, while imparting to it a distinctively political meaning. Within the terms of Peirce's logic of inquiry, every logical interpretant is a conjecture and 'every conjecture is equivalent to, or is expressive of, such a habit that having a certain desire one might accomplish it if one could perform a certain act'. More specifically, 'the species of future tense of the logical interpretant is that of the conditional mood, the "*would-be*"'. Thus,

> To predicate . . . [an intellectual] concept of a real or imaginary object is equivalent to declaring that a certain operation, corresponding to the concept, *if* performed upon that object, *would* (certainly, or probably, or possibly, according to the mode of predication) be followed by a result of a definite general description.[70]

To predicate is to predict. This is the relation to the 'absolute object', at the limit of infinite semiosis, that is established by final logical interpretants. Semiosis only remains endless outside of a practical orientation to the world. (Such is the intellectualism of deconstruction.) However, our practical relation to the world is experimental and hence fallible. The infinite semiosis of logical interpretants thus stands as a permanent background resource for new practical relations, to be tested in the world. Furthermore, this threefold dynamic of interpretive, pragmatic and (speculative or negative) ontological forms is as constitutive of the 'subject' as it is of the 'object' of knowledge. (The 'absolute object' will have to be an 'absolute subject' as well.) This is its cultural dimension.[71]

With its combination of speculative metaphysical realism and practical experimentation, this model bears a close resemblance to Benjamin's account of the joint role of perception and use in the appropriation of cultural forms: mastering the tasks facing 'the human apparatus of perception ... gradually by habit' by collective testing and communication of results.[72] Benjamin's adherence to a speculative metaphysical realism of the 'absolute object' ('history') aligns his cultural history with the ontological structure of Peirce's theory of interpretants, providing the level of mediation that is needed to turn semiotics into a 'logic of culture' – the aspiration of cultural studies since the 1970s. For the 'history of forms' that Barthes designated 'the essential aim of semiological research'[73] is not to be found at the level of signifying systems, but, more fundamentally, at that of the history of technologies of image production or signifying media. Furthermore, for Benjamin, while all images are historical indices, the historical character of the present is such that:

> The historical index of the images not only says that they belong to a particular time; it says, above all, that they attain to legibility only at a particular time. And, indeed, this acceding 'to legibility' constitutes a specific critical point in the movement at their interior. Every present day is determined by the images that are synchronic with it: each 'now' is the now of a particular recognizability.[74]

Benjamin's understanding of historical experience as a dialectical relationship between a 'now' and a 'then' internal to the interpretation of images, metonymically figuring history as a whole, gives to the hermeneutics of the 'final interpretant' an immanently speculative and hence critical turn.

For Peirce, the speculative limit of the absolute object is an abstract horizon, bordering an endless series; for Benjamin, it is to be grasped, albeit fleetingly, immanently to experience. For in 'the now of a particular recognizability' truth appears 'charged to the bursting point with time'. 'This point of explosion, and nothing else,' Benjamin continues, 'is the death of *intentio*, which thus coincides with the birth of authentic historical time, the time of truth.' Yet such an interruptive 'birth of time' is not itself temporal, or at least it is not durational, but, in its instantaneity, eternalizing and therefore spatial: 'For while the relation of the present to the past is purely temporal, the relation of what-has-been to the now is dialectical: not temporal in nature but figural *<bildlich>*.'[75] Within such an experience, instantaneity figures the timelessness of time as a whole. The photographic character of this experience could hardly be clearer; nor could its visceral quality, traversing logical, energetic and emotional interpretants. It is this visceral quality that allows it to perform its critical function of *putting the present into crisis*, in the literal sense of producing an awareness of the present as a turning-point, the possible ground of radically different futures. It is the 'suspension of habitual relationships among the elements of nature' (Kracauer) that this involves which is the 'habit' that Benjamin's cultural history aims to help instill.

If this mode of cultural history has itself finally 'acceded to legibility', it is perhaps because of the *passing* of the photograph as the technically dominant form of image production, consequent upon the increasing generalized use of digital technologies of imaging. The passing of the photograph makes the relationship between its indexical and its iconic functions – its unique existential character – increasingly visible today. The illusion of absolute analogy carried by the purely denotative aspect of the photographic image made it, for a hundred and fifty years, the epistemically privileged form of the image, to which other forms of image production had progressively to accommodate themselves in order to produce credible denotative effects. The continuous or 'all-over' image imposed by the technical form of the photographic process became a socio-historically imposed normative form of aesthetic totality to which other cultural forms (literary and visual) were tendentially subject.[76] Today the dominance of this form is in crisis. Nevertheless, a Benjaminian approach to cultural history offers us the possibility of conceptualizing this process, this crisis, in a way which is at once historical and metaphysical – free from semiotic and aesthetic idealisms alike – whereby the temporal-political significance or cultural-historical possibilities of the latest forms of image-production can be brought more clearly into view. In historizing and re-cognitivizing aesthetics through attention to the aesthetic dimension of technological form, Benjamin opens aesthetics out onto broader social processes without leaving behind the experience of form. It is the mediated historical character of what is nonetheless a speculative-existential philosophical form that distinguishes Benjamin's approach, in principle, from the otherwise affinitive metaphysical pragmatism of Deleuze.

Coda: and Deleuze?

Deleuze is the great white hope of a non-Saussurean cultural theory, offering the prospect of a new beginning.[77] His work not only contains philosophical and political criticisms of the semiotic and psychoanalytical assumptions of most recent cultural theory, it also provides a whole new problematic, with its own philosophical genealogy, distinctive set of concepts, terminology and modes of address. In particular, it involves an appropriation and transformation of Peirce's trichotomy of signs that claims to uncover its implicit political logic, while redescribing its metaphysical basis (the absolute as limit of infinite semiosis) in terms of the 'single plane of consistency' of the 'assemblages' of the social itself.[78] Is Deleuze, perhaps, the Benjamin of the day?[79]

In the light of the differences in cultural context and historical time, the correspondences between Benjamin's and Deleuze's writings are indeed striking. Each thinks out of a canon that includes Nietzsche-Bergson-Proust-Kafka on its central axis; each maintains a non-Hegelian concept of the absolute, while thematizing and seeking out 'the new'; each focuses on the image and its productive, affective and intensive charge; each understands film as the cultural dominant and point of view from which to philosophize; each maintains a privileged but idiosyncratic relationship to Marx's writings; and each emphasizes the radical openness of the real as the condition of politics. Such affinities are all the more striking for the distance they mark from most of what counts as cultural theorizing today. Yet for all the immanent dynamism of its metaphysical pragmatism or constructivism, Deleuze's thought remains plagued by a naturalism of desire ('the objective being of desire is the Real in and for itself')[80] that short-circuits both cultural-historical and political analysis in its protest against the 'territorializing' tendencies of the social as such. In this respect, in conceding the social, ontologically, to the rule of the sign, it opts out of the key problem – 'the nature of the socius to come'[81] – that provides cultural analysis with its motivating orientation and *raison d'être*. We can see this reduction at work in Deleuze's appropriation of Peirce.

Deleuze acknowledges Peirce as 'the true inventor' of semiotics, whose strength was 'to conceive of signs on the basis of images and their combinations, not as a function of determinants which are already linguistic'. Furthermore, Deleuze considers pragmatics, not as 'a complement to logic, syntax, or semantics', but, on the contrary, as 'the fundamental element upon which all the rest depend'. He thus follows Peirce in accepting that (a non-linguistic) semiotics will be a 'descriptive science of reality (logic)'. Images exist on the same ontological level as objects, as semiotically, aesthetically and pragmatically formed portions of matter.[82] Where Deleuze differs from Peirce is in his characterization of this level in terms of a positive, affirmative and productive notion of a desire which is at once immediately libidinal and yet moulded into social forms. This ontological characterization imparts to Peirce's three types of sign distinct ontologico-political meanings, while leading Deleuze to distinguish the diagram, in principle, from other types of sign, as a sign with 'neither substance nor form, neither content nor expression', but rather, the pure construction of a 'new type of reality'.[83] (For Peirce, the diagram was an icon of relation.)

Deleuze maps Peirce's semiotic trichotomy of icon, index and symbol onto a conception of the social as the coding or inscription of desire, an immanent process of the 'territorializing', 'deterritorializing' and 'reterritorializing' of desire by various 'desiring-machines'. For Deleuze, *everything* is 'desiring-production'; it is 'the essential reality of man and nature'. Such production takes the form of a 'flow' that is constantly interrupted, 'drained off' into partial objects, and reinstituted. 'Every "object" presupposes the continuity of a flow; every flow, the fragmentation of the object.' Machines (essentially, all organized and organizing structures, natural or social) 'cut into' these flows by coding them in various ways. We are thus presented with an internally differentiated monist ontology or libidinal economy in which 'what is' is *at once* pure multiplicity, 'an affirmation that is irreducible to any sort of unity', and a field of energy ordered into a structured but unstable network of signifying chains. Each aspect relies upon the other, since interruption is the condition of the renewal of the flow of desire ('signs produce desire') which, in turn, provides the material for the always partial 'segmentary' investments that define distinct strata and forms of life.[84]

Movements of territorialization quantify the 'assemblages' within different strata. Assemblages are at once 'machinic' (assemblages of 'bodies, of actions and passions') and 'enunciative' (collective assemblages of enunciation, of 'acts and statements, of incorporeal transformations attributed to bodies'). The specificity of the capitalist 'formation of sovereignty' within this ontology is taken to be that

> the great social axiomatic has replaced the territorial codes and the despotic overcoding that characterized the preceding formations; and a molar gregarious aggregate has formed whose mode of subjugation has no equal ... an unprecedented decoding and deterritorialization, which institutes a combination as a system of differential relations between the decoded and deterritorialized flows, in such a way that social inscription and repression no longer even need to bear directly upon bodies and persons, but on the contrary precede them ...

However, 'the great mutant flow of capital ... performs an equivalent reterritorialization when converted into a reflux of means of payment' (property). The 'capital-money socius' thus oscillates between the poles of two very different forms of desire.[85]

Within this framework, indices, icons and symbols are 'distinguished by territoriality-deterritorialization relations, not signifier-signified relations': *indices* are territorial signs or 'territorial states of things constituting the designatable', *icons* are 'operations of reterritorialization constituting the signifiable', and *symbols* 'pertain to relative or negative deterritorialization', in 'a constant movement of referral from sign to sign'.[86] These are immediately political categories, not in the general pragmatic sense that, for Peirce, the tense of logical interpretants is the future conditional, but because territorialization is both the form and the measure of the repression of desire. For the authors of *Anti-Oedipus*, 'one can never go far enough in the direction of deterritorialization'. *Anti-Oedipus* is an apocalyptic text, a prophetic libertarian utopianism of the 'overthrow of power' (territorialization) and the 'return of production itself to desire'. It imagines a point at which reterritorializations make the earth 'so artificial that the movement of deterritorialization creates of necessity and by itself a new earth . . . a world created in the process of its . . . coming undone.' Its slogan is thus '*Long live capital in all its reality, in all its objective dissimulation!*'[87]

Peirce's trichotomy thus furnishes Deleuze with the basis for an alternative political semiotics, mapping the social in terms of distinct 'regimes of signs'. The further innovation – the irreducibility of the diagram to either the icon or the symbol – functions to mark the moment of pure construction or creation, 'the constitution of potentiality', associated with that *absolute* deterritorialization which is the (impossible?) political correlate of the absolute itself. Diagrams are understood to produce, rather than to represent, relations. Deleuze names the agents of such deterritorialization 'abstract machines'. They are attributed the potentiality 'to extract and accelerate destratified particles-signs (the passage to the absolute)'. Such particles-signs are understood to 'constitute unformed traits capable of combining with one another. This is the height of abstraction, but also the moment at which abstraction becomes real; everything operates through abstract-real machines'. Abstract machines are effectuated in the 'concrete assemblages' of the social and have no existence outside them – a type of being for which Marx's analysis of the money-form acts as the model.[88]

This is a full-blown, systematic, metaphysical and semiotic pragmatism.[89] In it, Deleuze *appears* to have socialized, historized, politicized, and hence de-realized, the static metaphysical ground of Peirce's pragmatism (the 'absolute object' as the limit of infinite semiosis). However, his position is in crucial respects more, not less, naturalistic than Peirce's. For Deleuze neglects the theory of interpretants, and with it, the semiotic specificity of the subject of habitual action. From the beginning, he misreads Peirce through the Saussurean model he himself rejects. For in Peirce, icon, index and symbol are *not* 'distinguished by signifier-signified relations'. This is Saussure's (Stoic) terminology. They characterize a sign's relations to its 'object' (an ambiguous term, embracing both the 'immediate' and the 'dynamic' object) not its 'signified'. Signification is a triadic relation, requiring an interpretant, not a two-way, signifier-signifed one. Consequently, it is not just the symbol which is open to 'a constant movement of referral from sign to sign', but *all* signs; all signs, that is, outside their subjection to a final interpretant.

When Deleuze does refer to Peirce's distinction between Firstness, Secondness and Thirdness, in the first of his *Cinema* volumes, he transposes it into a distinction between types of image: affection-image, action-image, and mental-image.[90] This is confusing in a number of respects; not least, because in Peirce all three are required as necessary conditions and aspects of *any* signification. One would need to speak of the different weightings of the affective, active and mental aspects of every image. The idea that there are 'affection-images, in the strict sense ... [that] only refer to firstness' is incoherent. Firstness is the aesthetic quality of the image, but there is no purely aesthetic signification. That is the founding insight of semiotics. Thus, when Deleuze writes that 'the close-up retains the ... power to tear the image away from spatio-temporal coordinates in order to call forth the pure affect as the expressed',[91] the very idea of the expressed introduces a Secondness, its 'object'. 'Pure affect' is the object (second) of affection images. Or when he writes that it was 'Hitchcock's task to introduce the mental image into the cinema ... In Hitchcock, actions, affections, perceptions, all is interpretation',[92] he is calling attention to the density of semiotic relations between the images within the films, their potential to act as interpretants for each other. (Formally, any sign can act as an interpretant for another sign.) More problematic still is Deleuze's neglect of the notion of the final interpretant, which grounds the interpretive process, pragmatically, giving shape to what would otherwise be an indeterminate and infinite semiosis. For Peirce final logical interpretants (interpretants of intellectual or general signs) are changes of habit. With the notion of habit, Peirce's semiotics might be thought to rejoin Deleuze's pragmatism. However, as we saw with regard to Eco's reductively behavioural reading of habit, Peirce's concept of habit resists a completely naturalistic interpretation. This remains true, despite the subtleties of Deleuze's Bergsonian naturalism.

Peirce's association of convention with 'habit and acquired law' in his definition of the symbol (in distinction from the Saussurean conflation of convention with arbitrariness in the linguistic sign), opens up a space for the naturalization of convention, indeed, for an evolutionary semiotic naturalism. Hence its attraction for Deleuze, for whom Bergson's *Creative Evolution* was a fundamental point of reference. However, for Peirce this process is *subjectively mediated* at various different levels of inference, in such a way as to free the formation of habit from dependence on repetition. Deleuze recognizes that habit relates to contemplation, rather than being a mechanical relationship between actions, but he retains the relation to repetition, since, ultimately for him, 'contemplation' is itself a bodily act, an act of 'contraction' constituting the self.

> When we say that habit is a contraction we are speaking not of
> an instantaneous action which combines with another to form an

element of repetition, but rather of the fusion of that repetition in the contemplating mind. A soul must be attributed to the heart, to the muscles, nerves and cells, but a contemplative soul whose entire function is to contract a habit.[93]

For Peirce, on the other hand, while signs produce desire, they also reproduce subjects, as more than mere effects, since they mediate transactions between subjects and the world within the horizon of the 'absolute object'. Such mediations are different in principle from other habits of nature, since they have a *social* logic in which communicative and other practical relations are articulated in an ontologically distinctive way. This is the missing dimension of Deleuze's thought. Furthermore, politically, is it not the *breaking* of habits that we are concerned with (initially, at least): the production of a desire to become another kind of subject, to live another kind of life?

The breaking of habit is the interruptive function of the static quality of the photograph and dialectical images more generally – Kracauer's 'suspension of every habitual relationship' – although, of course, such suspension can itself become habitual, which deepens the pragmatics of modernity. For Deleuze, however, such passing deterritorializations are judged 'negative' if linked to some projected reterritorialization, however creative or abstract. It is at this point that the contradiction between the political intent and ontological structure of Deleuze's thought becomes unsustainable. The *immediately* political character of Deleuze's categories (seductive for that type of cultural studies that would conceive itself as immediately political)[94] becomes an alibi for the failure to think radical politics as a social project, consequent upon treating the social field as such, ultimately, as the power to be overturned. Two admirers of Deleuze express this difficulty as follows: he and Guattari

> seem to be able to conceive positively only the tendencies toward continuous movement and absolute flows, and thus . . . the creative elements and the radical ontology of the production of the social remain insubstantial and impotent. [They] discover the productivity of social reproduction (creative production, production of values, social relations, affects, becomings), but manage to articulate it only superficially and ephemerally, as a chaotic, indeterminate horizon marked by an ungraspable event.[95]

Yet this is no failure of articulation or resolve. It follows logically from the structure of the ontology: 'the plane of consistency knows nothing of substance and form'. Indeed, this is its point.[96] Yet mediation, and the specificity of the social, are the very space of cultural analysis, both conceptually and pragmatically. In so far as it has a political project of its own, disjunctive but articulated with politics in its wider sense, cultural studies aims to help foster 'new kinds of authority', new habits, that will '*matter, in this world, in future*'.[97]

Conceptual productivity is the *leitmotif* of Deleuze's concept of philosophy.[98] Yet, in a situation in which philosophical and empirical concepts co-exist on the same ontological plane, without mediation, it is at times too easily confused with terminological productivity or inventive redescription – as the occasional degeneration of both *A Thousand Plateaus* and the *Cinema* volumes into self-enclosed baroque worlds of neologized taxonomies of signs shows. In so far as it lacks the mediation of specifically social and historical concepts, Deleuze's naturalism is at once a form of empiricism (positing the immediately given as real) and of philosophism (positing the immediate reality of philosophical concepts), for which the idea of a 'transcendental empiricism' provides merely terminological cover. Badiou's reading of Deleuze may self-servingly reduce him to the parameters of his own philosophical classicism,[99] but as *What is Philosophy?* shows, Deleuze was by no means averse to such disciplinary classicism himself – albeit of a rather different variety to Badiou's.

This is not to suggest that Deleuze's work contains nothing of value for cultural theory. Far from it. The critique of the familialism of psychoanalysis in *Anti-Oedipus*, for example, is devastating, and requires of it fundamental theoretical reconstruction;[100] while the (inadvertent?) narrative mediations regulating the relations between the *auteur* criticism of the cinema volumes and its baroque semiotic metaphysics open up multiple directions for future work. But it does suggest that it is singularly inappropriate as the philosophical basis for a new paradigm. Rather, at its best, it is as a deviant practice – a kind of philosophical 'minor literature'[101] – that Deleuze's writing excels, subverting classical philosophical discourse from within its *own* language, by using it in newly direct and unexpected ways.

3

MODERNISM AS
TRANSLATION

It is the theoretical virtue of comparative cultural study that it forces us to rethink the abstract opposition of 'philosophical' to 'empirical' concepts by focusing on the conceptual semantics and socio-political dynamics of processes of generalization of particular terms. What is, could be, or should be, the status of the most general concepts of a genuinely 'transnational' cultural theory? And what is the relationship of their forms of universality to other, philosophical and empirical, conceptual forms? To what extent do the theoretical prehistory and process of formation of such concepts impinge upon their use in the present? In particular, is there any way in which such concepts can avoid the fate of becoming little more than intellectual markers, or even symbolic enhancers, of global processes of cultural domination and hegemony? Indeed, can or should there be general concepts – concepts of sufficient generality to embrace the full geopolitical range of a genuinely transnational cultural theory – at all? Alternatively, can there be transnational cultural theory without them?

These are live questions, in the sense of being both urgent and unresolved questions, open questions, which trouble the otherwise implacable progress of the competing yet overlapping problematics that make up the field of cultural theory today: problematics for which the labels 'postcolonialism', 'postmodernism', 'globalization', 'critical anthropology', 'new ethnography', and even 'cultural studies' itself stand in as so many shorthand markers, marketing thoughts in progress as finished products: off-the-shelf items, ready-to-wear, in the new international supermarkets of knowledge. These are in many ways unhappy problematics. Yet, together, they represent a vast and complex field of writing and research which is fundamentally transforming the conceptual landscape of disciplines in the humanities and social sciences – not least, via a recognition of the inextricability of economic and cultural processes and practices.

This chapter approaches these questions, first, via a translational model of theoretical generality and, second, through a reconsideration of the logic of the concept of modernism – from the standpoint of a conception of philosophy as speculative totalization through cross-disciplinary critique.

However, to address these questions from such a standpoint is not necessarily the same thing as addressing them from 'within' philosophy, since 'what philosophy is', as they say in the undergraduate primers in Western universities, is one of the things at stake in the discussion. What might philosophy become?[1]

The question of the status of the terms of a transnational cultural theory opens onto the question of the status of philosophical concepts in two ways: 1) as a question about the cultural-historical constitution and hence *limits to universality* of all thought and 2) as a question about the productive *transcendence* of thinking beyond both the conditions of its own possibility and the range of its currently empirically justifiable applications. This is the transcendence of the present towards the future, that is, *finite* transcendence, in the early Heideggerian sense; transcendence towards the being-in-common of a 'finite history'.[2] The concept of modernism is paradigmatic in this regard, as a Western cultural form subsequently generalized at a global level in a hotly disputed process suspended between the imperialism of an obliteration of social differences and the productivity of alternative, counter-hegemonic interpretations and conceptions. Either way, the meaning of the concept has undoubtedly been transformed by its extension to 'non-Western' contexts, situations and instances, while nonetheless retaining a certain highly abstract, but still recognizable, shape. Furthermore, modernism is in certain respects directly akin to a traditional philosophical concept in designating the cultural affirmation of a particular phenomenological structure of time. That is to say, it is a concept belonging to a phenomenological philosophy of history, as well as, at lower levels of abstraction, to empirical-typological histories of cultural forms.[3]

I shall return to the logic of modernism as a philosophical concept shortly. First, however, let us consider the translational model of theoretical generality which underlies the practice of theory construction in much contemporary cultural study. For it is in its function as a medium of translation, I shall argue, that the concept of modernism maintains a certain legitimate universality as a generic concept of a transnational cultural theory.

A translational model of theoretical generality

One increasingly common way in which the process of theoretical generalization is understood in cultural theory is through the metaphor – or at least, what looks at first sight like a metaphor – of translation. Theoretically, however, translation may be understood in any of a number of different ways. It is the theory of translation underlying the use of the idea of comparative analysis as a process of translation which determines the philosophical meaning of the concepts concerned. Take, for example, this passage from the prologue to a recent book by James Clifford, *Routes: Travel and Translation in the Late Twentieth Century* (1997), in which he is discussing the status of comparative concepts in cultural theory:

> All broadly meaningful concepts, terms such as 'travel,' are translations, built from imperfect equivalences. To use comparative concepts in a situated way means to become aware, always belatedly, of limits, sedimented meanings, tendencies to gloss over differences. Comparative concepts – translation terms – are approximations, privileging certain 'originals' and made for specific audiences. Thus, the broad meanings that enable projects such as mine [rethinking spatiality as itinerary – an immanent temporalization of a specific set of spatial relations] necessarily fail as a consequence of whatever range they achieve. This mix of success and failure is a common predicament for those attempting to think globally – globally enough – without aspiring to overview and the final word.[4]

This passage is exemplary in its use of the idea of translation to instil a certain postmodern scepticism into the heart of comparative analysis. On the one hand, it is admirably epistemologically cautious: it associates the empirical specificity of contextual self-consciousness with an awareness of 'limits, sedimented meanings, [and] tendencies to gloss over differences'. On the other hand, however, it extends and hypostasizes this caution into the 'necessary failure' of all 'broad meanings'. (But failure to do what? According to what criteria?) What begins as a practically-based care about context turns into a scepticism about theoretical concepts in general. The concept of translation which was used, to begin with, to open up the field of comparative generality, is turned back upon that field and closes it down. The hinge of this movement is the idea of the 'privilege of the original'. It is the primacy of the original context, in which the concept is seen to be 'made for specific audiences', which, for Clifford, dictates the 'failure' which necessarily accompanies whatever success in translation there may be.

Yet one might very well question the model of translation underlying this view. For rather than using the idea of translation to extend and thereby *transform* the meaning of theoretical concepts through their application to new contexts, Clifford's use of the idea of the 'privilege of the original' insulates such concepts from the very contexts which would change them. What we have here, in fact, is a traditional anthropological model in which the 'other' is assumed to be preconstituted in its otherness prior to the encounter, thereby establishing an *a priori* limit to the possibility of translation. But is this what cultural alterity and translation are actually like? There are good conceptual grounds for thinking not. For not only is the 'otherness of the other' a dialectical *product* of the encounter – that is, something to be inferred from the necessity for translation, rather than the preestablished ground of its inevitable failure[5] – but the meaning of 'the original' cannot be supposed to reside wholly 'within' the original itself. Given the increased range and intensity of the social exchanges which have made the idea of a transnational cultural theory both necessary and possible, one might do better to consider the alternative model of translation contained in Walter Benjamin's notion of the 'translatability' of the original.

For Benjamin,

> [t]ranslatability is an essential quality of certain works, which is not to say that it is essential that they be translated; it means rather that a specific significance inherent in the original manifests itself in its translatability . . . The life of originals attains in [translations] to its ever-renewed latest and most abundant flowering.[6]

Indeed,

> no translation would be possible if in its ultimate essence it strove for likeness to the original. For in its afterlife – which could not be called that if it were not a transformation and a renewal of something living – the original undergoes a change. Even a word with fixed meaning can undergo a maturing process . . . [A] translation, instead of resembling the meaning of the original must lovingly and in detail incorporate the original's mode of signification, thus making both the original and the translation recognizable as fragments of a greater language, just as fragments are part of a vessel.

In this way, all significant works of translation extend the boundaries of the language into which they translate.[7]

The relevant questions thus become: What is the 'mode of signification' of the original? What 'specific significance' is manifest in its translatability? And what changes does it undergo as a consequence of particular translations?

At the time of this essay, in 1923, Benjamin still conceived of this process in only weakly historical terms, as a process of the concealment and revelation of a metaphysical 'language of truth':

> the tensionless and even silent depository of the ultimate truth which all thought strives for . . . the true language . . . whose divination and description is the only perfection a philosopher can hope for . . . concealed in concentrated fashion in translations.[8]

However, one may reinterpret it in the spirit of Benjamin's later, more deeply historical conception of construction in order to develop it as a basis for the theorization of the mode of generality of the concepts of a transnational cultural theory. On such a model, the process of translation would be a reflective part of the broader historical process of construction which *produces* the 'truth' which the early Benjamin tended to see, in quasi-Platonic terms, as already implicit. After all, what is conceptual determination but a re-presentation as 'universality' of the immanent ideality of a historically produced and sedimented, yet necessarily incomplete and hence speculative, generality? There is a dialectic of universal and particular – conceptual determination and empirical particularity – internal to all theoretical concepts as a consequence of their historicity. In this respect, the idea of translation at work in cultural theory (general concepts as 'translation terms' or media of translation) is less a metaphor than the metonymic register of the interpretative dimension of the processes of social intercourse and exchange in general. As Derrida has put it: 'With the problem of translation we are dealing with nothing less than the passage to philosophy' – that is, with the question of the possibility of universality in discourse.[9]

So, how does 'modernism' function as a translation term? What is its mode of signification? What specific significance is manifest in its translatability? And what changes does it undergo as a consequence of its translation into 'non-Western' – for example, Chinese – contexts?

Modernism as a philosophical concept

In its broadest sense and most fundamental theoretical determination 'modernism' displays the universality of a philosophical concept. This is not to deny that modernism is a historical and hence in part a sociological phenomenon – the name for an historically emergent and hence derived form of historical self-consciousness, associated with a specific range of cultural objects and practices, in particular kinds of society – or that it comes in many guises. Rather, in comparing 'modernism' to a philosophical concept, I wish simply to draw attention to its transcendental or quasi-categorial status as a temporal form, across and within the particular modes of historical life in which it is found, and to the peculiar kind of universality inherent in the radical abstractness of this form. More specifically, as the name for the *cultural affirmation of a particular temporal logic of negation* ('the new', the temporal logic of the modern), modernism is the cultural condition of possibility of a particular, distinctively future-oriented series of forms of experience of history as temporal form. The questions raised by this for a transnational cultural theory are: How is this temporal logic of negation produced and played out under different, but always related, social and historical conditions, at the level of particular cultural forms?

And what kinds of relation does it enter into with whatever might be taken to fall under the increasingly dubious heading of 'national cultures'?

I am opting, then, for an expansive definition of 'modernism'. In its most basic or core temporal sense, its reference cannot be restricted in advance either to the social domain of the arts, or to some chronologically bounded historical period (that is, one which has already ended), or to any particular geopolitical space (such as 'the West'). Rather, modernism is in principle 'aesthetic' only in the technical sense of the Transcendental Aesthetic in Kant's *Critique of Pure Reason*, where aesthetic is the name for the 'doctrine of sensibility' and transcendental aesthetic is 'the science of all principles of *a priori* sensibility' – that is, the pure forms of intuition: space and time.[10] Such a usage is no looser than more extensionally restricted definitions, although it is more abstract; no more abstract, though, than the aspect of actuality which it grasps. Such abstractness both registers the *actually existing temporal formalism* of 'the modern' as a structure of time-consciousness, or what Foucault would have called an historical *a priori*, and is the condition for its translatability into an increasing number of different geopolitical contexts. Similarly to labour-power, one might say, the modern is a real abstraction. It is in the distinctive and contradictory features of the mode of abstraction of the modern, and their relations to the concrete multiplicity of its empirical forms, that the specific significance of the translatability of 'modernism' resides.

More specifically, as the name for a structure of experience which is both categorial (that is, provides a functional unity of representations) and intuitive (that is, a form of affection), 'the modern' is *schematic* in Kants's precise sense of offering 'a rule of pure synthesis' or a 'transcendental determination of time' which mediates the relation of appearances to categorial forms – 'a monogram of pure imagination' in Kant's evocative phrase.[11] As a practical affirmation of the historical schema of 'the modern', modern*ism* is thus what we might call *a practical historical schema*. As such, it structures the temporal form of subjectivity, the temporality of the 'I', through its mediation of culturally received (intuited) temporal forms with new acts of production. It is for this reason that modernism in its most general sense is associated with a particular configuration of *temporalizations of history* or *historizations of temporality*.[12]

As I have said, by emphasizing the philosophical dimension of the concept of modernism, I do not wish to imply that it is independent of history either in its origins or immanently, within itself. Rather, it raises in a particular instance the general question of the relationship of philosophical to historical form. However, in insisting on the quasi-categorial status of modernism, in its most fundamental determination, as a name for the affirmations of a particular form of time-determination, I am attempting to free myself from the restrictions of the dominant empirical-typological conceptions of modernism in literary and art history, which are so often the given of sociological analysis in this area: that is, the conception of modernism as a particular, chronologically-defined, period style.[13] Different versions of this conception are still hegemonic in recent writings on the subject, for all their additional theoretical or sociological sophistication.[14] But they miss what is most fundamental about modernism: namely, its character as a temporal dynamic of cultural form. In particular, one might note 1) that the use of chronological periodization is in tension with the radically temporalizing character of the phenomenon in question, and 2) that the restriction to style, in conjunction with some more sociological notion of modernism as a self-conscious cultural movement, fails to come to grips with either the pervasiveness or the contradictory complexity of modernism as a cultural form. Indeed, the translatability of 'modernism' – the power of modernism as a medium of transculturation, one might say[15] – indicates the extent to which the concept can be unified, ultimately, *only* at the level of pure temporal form.

However, the point of criticizing such typological-stylistic analyses is not to side-step the empirical multiplicity of modernisms as a complex and developing set of concrete historical forms, by retreating to some self-contained realm of philosophical abstraction. Rather, the aim is to establish the terms for rethinking this material from the standpoint of the more fundamental determination of modernism as a temporal-cultural form, and thereby, to acquire a more adequate sense of its specifically *historical* (rather than either merely chronological or abstractly temporal) logic. For if we understand by modernism the cultural affirmation of a particular temporal logic of negation (the new), the meaning of any particular such negation will be determined by the delimitation of the received cultural field upon which, and within which, it acts. The specification of what delimits or gives conceptual unity to the field of a particular practical negation, and the level at which that negation operates, will constitute the varying historical significances of different, historically and geographically specific, 'modernisms'. These are, if you like, the terms of the translation, which reveal the 'specific significance' of modernism, manifest in its translatability – a significance which is most visible in its translation into 'non-Western' contexts. For it is at this point that the issue of difference enters the picture as the question of the status of the various forms of classification – of conceptual unity and division – which are involved in constituting the various fields of negation which make up the shifting object-domains of modernist culture.

If modernism has the universality of a philosophical concept, then – a concept constructed at the level of a certain phenomenologically *absolute* (albeit historically conditioned) universality – it nonetheless derives its concrete meaning from the distributive unity of its specific instances, as a particular constellation of fields of negation, at any particular time.

Hence its potentially contradictory manifestations in, for example, both radically nationalistic and radically anti-nationalistic, cosmopolitan forms, in different historical and national contexts, or, according to different political projects within the same historical and national context. This is dependent upon whether its field of negation is constituted internally or externally to the idea of 'national culture'.

Modernism and national culture

Whatever 'national culture' may be, there can be no conceptually necessary relationship between it and modernism as a cultural form, specifiable in advance. There are only historically specific conjunctural relations, constructed by the (politically defined) terms of identification of particular fields of negation. In particular, one can make no legitimate inferences from the founding conjunction of specific canonic modernisms with particular national projects to the possibility or impossibility of other forms. Indeed, the 'national' character of specific modernisms is often national in a dialectical sense only, as determinate negations of received national-cultural forms: internally oppositional cosmopolitan projections, only later put to hegemonizing nationalistic use. Rather, at base, the concept of modernism offers a general interpretative framework for identifying and examining the carriers of a specific form of time-determination – a specific temporal logic of negation – across and between different social and cultural fields. This is true, although the distance from traditional cultural forms registered by this radical temporal abstraction does indeed associate it with a particular culture – the culture of capital – which exists unevenly within the cultural formations of capitalist societies. (Paradigmatically, of course, commodity culture is 'made in the USA', where the 'national' tradition is more inherently capitalistic than elsewhere.) As such, it is of increasing and not decreasing global relevance. This should not, however, be taken to imply that the political content of any particular modernism is in some way compromised by this affinity, in advance, since the social embodiment of its abstract temporal logic – what is being affirmed – might be quite different from that from which that logic evolved, historically.

It is thus mistaken, in my view, to think of 'Chinese modernism', for example, in painting and film, as culturally specific variants or exotic indigenous inflections of medium-specific modernisms conceptually defined in formal-stylistic terms by their Western counterparts – as both Alice Yang and Xudong Zhang still tend to do, in different ways, for all their reflectivity about the structure of 'othering' constitutive of such Western modernisms.[16] The implications of the translation of 'modernism' into the context of China are far more complicated than that. In temporal terms, Soviet-style Socialist Realism is a far more credible candidate for the role of an inaugural modernism in Chinese painting than any extension of the formalism of its traditional visual culture,[17] just as the dynamics of revolutionary-socialist state-led modernization constitute at least as important a part of its specific modernity as do either market relations or any more nationally specific cultural traits. Unfortunately, we still lack anything approaching an adequate theorization of socialist modernity as a cultural-historical form.

This power of generalization has nothing, at base, to do with any generic autonomy of philosophical concepts; although, internationally, concepts like modernism have become generalized cultural resources. Rather, it follows from the global generalization of the various dynamics of social transformation which underlie the time-consciousness of modernism as an affirmative (and often in some sense 'alternative') cultural project: namely, the various articulations of economic, social-geographic, and inter-state logics which determine the rhythm of 'modernity' as a condition of change. The only thing that is distinctive about 'modernism' as a cultural form, *per se* – prior to its translational specification – is that the modes of identification which it designates involve a rupturally *futural* sense of the present as an (always, in part, destructive) transition to a (temporary) new order. Such is its abstract universality, as distinct from the concrete universality which is the historical product of the development of its increasingly generalized empirical forms. The problem is thus not how to rethink the notion of modernism from the standpoint of national cultures (modernism as national allegory, for example). It is, rather, how the problematic of the modern, concretely applied, can help *replace* the problematic of 'national cultures', with a broader conception of the temporal-cultural dimensions of social relations – social relations through which 'the nation' is itself produced as a cultural-ideological effect of various forms of state power.[18]

The changes that the concept of modernism undergoes as a result of its translation into 'non-Western' contexts are changes of reference (and hence, in Benjamin's account of translation, enrichments of sense) consequent upon its association with a radically extended range of forms of cultural experience of temporal difference or non-synchronicity. These new forms of production of 'the modern' fracture its identification with its Euro-American 'original', retrospectively transforming that original in turn. Furthermore, if we understand space as 'the material support of time-sharing social practices', and 'globalization' as the planetary extension of such practices made possible by the new information technologies,[19] it is clear that questions about 'non-Western' modernities and modernisms can no longer be separated from questions about a global modernity and globally projected modernisms – not simply because of the enforced generalization of European and American models of development (through colonialism and imperialism), but because of the opening up of more generalized spaces of translation in the 'real virtuality' of what Castells

61

calls the 'space of flows'. Although, as Castells is quick to point out, these new forms of communicational relations often exist in active contradiction to the political dynamics of the more established 'space of places'.

If the question 'What is modern, now?' which underlies all modernisms, is asked in these circumstances, it will be spatially double-coded as: 1) What is modern, here and now (in this *place* – city, province, nation, region, continent)?; and 2) What is modern now, *tout court* or globally? It is in the increasingly complex exchange between these two questions – an exchange through which West/non-West relations are currently being radically transformed – that the full scope of modernism as a term of translation manifests itself, as the name for the temporal form through which the political contest between competing futures continues to be played out.

4

REMEMBER THE FUTURE?

The *Communist Manifesto* as cultural-historical form

Modernism is a term of translation, across space and across time, linking together a wide variety of practices on the basis of a common temporal form. As such it is at once determined by and determining of these practices, in a dialectic internal to its conceptual form. At a time in which the context of the concept of modernism grows ever more global, embracing new and often surprising instances, it is fitting to revisit the founding text of an internationalist political modernism, now over one hundred and fifty years years old: Marx's and Engels' *Communist Manifesto*.

The *Communist Manifesto* is without doubt the most influential single text written in the nineteenth century, in any language, by some considerable way. Translated into thirty-five langauges, it appeared in 544 separate editions prior to 1918, at which point its dissemination accelerated so rapidly that even the most dedicated Marxologists lost count.[1] Indeed, the *Manifesto* may stand as a metonym for the desire called 'history' which coursed through that century in the wake of the French Revolution. Situated at the hinge between Hobsbawm's ages of revolution and capital (1789–1848 and 1848–1870), as described in the first two volumes of his great trilogy on the long nineteenth century, from the French Revolution to the First World War,[2] the *Communist Manifesto* presents the historical dialectic between these two terms ('revolution' and 'capital') in two equally extraordinary, but no longer equally convincing, ways: from the standpoint of the prospectively successive revolutionary historical roles of two social classes, bourgeoisie and proletariat, respectively. The disjunction between these two presentations must form the starting-point for any reconsideration of the meaning of the text today. For with the disappearance of the horizon of proletarian revolution as a political event on a world scale, and the retreat to the spirit- or dream-world of the famous 'spectre' of communism, the text has undergone a profound transformation. In short, the *Manifesto* appears to have been transformed from an eschatological *tour de force*, in which the end of capitalism was assured ('What the bourgeoisie ... produces, above all, is its own gravediggers'), into what Marshall Berman has notoriously described as a 'lyrical celebration of bourgeois works':[3] a celebration, more specifically, of the *revolutionary temporality* of capitalism; a capitalism which – without a fundamental countervailing political force – appears now as open-ended.

From the standpoint of the philosophy of history, communism as the eschatological absolute has given way to the 'bad infinity' of capitalism – 'the affirmation as negation of the finite'[4] – capitalism without end, amen. There has been a radical reversal in the historical meaning of the text. Thus has a shape of life grown old, freeing philosophy, once again, to 'paint its grey on grey'. Or at least, so it would seem. But does the politics of the *Manifesto* itself belong unambiguously to that shape of life, or is it still part of what Mephistopheles – in the passage from Goethe's *Faust* from which Hegel took his famous image – calls 'life's golden tree'?[5] Is the *Communist Manifesto* still a 'living' political text, after the fall of historical communism? If so how, or in what way? Is there, perhaps, *new* life in it today? What lives in the *Communist Manifesto*? In particular – and this is my topic in this chapter – what is the temporal character of its address to us, citizen-subjects of Western capitalist democracies? How does it inscribe us into historical time, today?

The poetry of transition

Let me quote what is probably – in the wake of Marshal Berman's path-breaking work – the most cited passage from the *Communist Manifesto*, in a Western academic context, over the last fifteen years (in Samuel Moore's translation of 1888):

> The bourgeoisie, historically, has played a most revolutionary part. The bourgeoisie, wherever it has got the upper hand, has put an end to all feudal, patriarchal, idyllic relations. It has pitilessly torn asunder the motley feudal ties that bound men and women to their 'natural superiors', and has left remaining no other nexus between people than naked self-interest, than callous 'cash payment'. It has drowned the most heavenly ecstasies of religious fervour, of chivalrous enthusiasm, of philistine sentimentalism, in the icy waters of egotistical calculation. It has resolved personal worth into exchange value, and in place of the numberless inde-feasible chartered freedoms, has set up that single, unconscionable freedom – Free Trade. In one word, for exploitation, veiled by religious and political illusions, it has substituted naked, shame-less, direct brutal exploitation ... [The bourgeoisie] has been the first to show what human activity can bring about. It has accom-plished wonders far surpassing Egyptian pyramids, Roman

aqueducts, and Gothic cathedrals; it has conducted expeditions that put in the shade all former Exoduses of nations and crusades.

And now, what is for Berman the most important part:

> The bourgeoisie cannot exist without constantly revolutionising the instruments of production, and thereby the relations of production, and with them the whole relations of society. Conservation of the old modes of production in unaltered form, was, on the contrary, the first condition of existence for all earlier industrial classes. Constant revolutionising of production, uninterrupted disturbance of all social conditions, everlasting uncertainty and agitation distinguish the bourgeois epoch from all earlier ones. All fixed, fast-frozen relations, with their train of ancient and venerable prejudices and opinions, are swept away, all new-formed ones become antiquated before they can ossify. All that is solid melts into air, all that is holy is profaned, and men and women are at last compelled to face with sober senses, their real conditions of life, and their relations with their kind.[6]

More specifically, according to Marx in the passage which follows, this 'constant revolutionising' has three main effects: economic and cultural globalization; subjection of the countryside to the towns; and political centralization in the form of new state-led or state-created nations. What is this but – as Berman describes it in the subtitle of his fine book – 'the experience of modernity'?

The culture of capital is the systemic instantiation of a Mephistophelean spirit of negation. And what is the *Communist Manifesto* from the standpoint of such a negation – a *Manifesto* without belief in the world-historical agency of the working classes, and with an acknowledgement of the powers of states and capitals to displace the effects of what had appeared to Marx as ultimately unmanageable crises; what is the *Communist Manifesto* in this context – in which the 'sorcerer' of modern society has regained a certain crucial measure of control over its powers – but, as Berman puts it, 'the archetype of a century of modernist manifestos and movements to come ... the first great modernist work of art'?[7]

When, in his Preface to the 1893 Italian edition of the *Manifesto*, Engels wrote of Dante as 'both the last poet of the Middle Ages and the first poet of modern times', in order to conjure the prospect of the 'new Dante, who will mark the hour of birth of this new proletarian era', he was appealing to national sentiment in Italy. Yet it is hard to read this passage without imputing a reference (if only unconscious) to Marx and to the *Manifesto* itself. However, if the era that was approaching was not in fact a proletarian one, but rather one of capitalism on a global scale, what does the Marx of the *Manifesto* become, if not *the poet of the transition to capitalism* (this is basically Berman's reading), a prefiguration in epic mode of Baudelaire and Flaubert?

As Berman argues, the rhythm of the *Manifesto*'s prose is driven by, and expresses in dissident form, a relentless temporal logic of negation – a 'revolutionary' logic – which derives, historically, from the logic of capital itself. Once the historically specific political demands of the *Manifesto* are set aside or judged to be superseded, it would seem, it cannot but appear (as it appears to Berman) in its pure modernist form, as an *identification with*, and *will to*, this abstract temporal logic itself. As I argued in the previous chapter, in its most fundamental determination, modernism simply *is* the cultural affirmation of the abstract temporal logic of negation.[8] Think, for example, of the first great Russian Futurist Manifesto of 1912, the Hylaea group's wonderfully entitled *Slap in the Face of Public Taste*, with the second of its 'orders' regarding poets' rights: the right to 'feel an insurmountable hatred for the language existing before their time'. Or of the yearning, at once theoretically abstract and phenomenologically concrete, expressed in the great concluding sentence of the first *Manifesto of Surrealism* (1924): 'Existence is elsewhere'.[9]

The 'melting vision' of Berman's modernist Marx extends beyond the specific futurities of qualitative historical novelty in the name of which manifestos are written (be they communist, futurist, or surrealist), to a generalized existential modernism that dissolves political subjectivity into the movement of time itself. Berman's Marx is, in this respect, rather surprisingly, something of a poststructuralist Marx. (Less surprisingly, perhaps, once one recognizes the disavowed roots of poststructuralism in existentialism.) This is a modernism which celebrates in *ecstatic* fashion

> the glory of modern energy and dynamism, the ravages of modern disintegration and nihilism, the strange intimacy between them; the sense of being caught in a vortex where all facts and values are whirled, exploded, decomposed, recombined; a basic uncertainty about what is basic, what is valuable, even what is real; a flaring up of the most radical hopes in the midst of their radical negations.[10]

'Time is everything, man is nothing; at the most, he is the carcase of time. Quality no longer matters' – as Marx himself put it in *The Poverty of Philosophy*, summing up the standpoint of what he called 'the fact of modern industry'.[11]

There is a powerful existential dimension to the *Communist Manifesto*, a particular quality of *futurity*, which, as Berman recognizes, belies the sociological schematism and historical stagism of its account of classes and modes of production. Berman's reading focuses on this dimension. Indeed, it celebrates it. Yet it also dehistoricizes it – takes the history out

of it – in a very particular way. It dehistoricizes its futurity, its identification with qualitative *historical* novelty, by reducing it to the abstract
temporal logic of negation of a generalized modernity. Indeed, paradoxically, it dehistoricizes it (the quality of its futurity) in the very act of
purporting to explain it, historically, as the cultural affect of a particular
form of social time: the time of the expanded reproduction of capital, the
revolutionary temporality of the bourgeoisie. The impulse towards a
different future, a *non-capitalist* future, is thus evacuated from the text,
not merely by Berman's notorious neglect of its historical argumentation
(the narrative of social contradiction and class struggle), but at the level
of its temporal-existential form as well. Berman's reading partakes in the
dehistoricizing movement of the purely existentialist, heroic modernism
which it purports to explain. (One thinks of Foucault's restricted
Baudelairean definition of modernism as 'the will to heroize'.)[12] Yet what
meaning can the qualitative historical novelty of Marx's 'we shall have'
possess, today – 'In place of the old bourgeois society, with its classes
and class antagonisms, *we shall have* an association, in which the free
development of each is the condition for the free development of all' –
when the narrative horizon of socialist revolution has disappeared from
the narrative of history? What meaning can it have except, as Berman
implies, that of an abstractly energizing hope, circulating within the closed
walls of the disintegrative turbulence of capitalist societies themselves? Or
to put the same question another way: from where else, historically –
from where else but capital – might the existential force and political
meaning of the *Manifesto* derive?

One way to approach this question is through a more detailed analysis
of the text as a cultural-historical form – that is, through an alternative
account of the *Manifesto*'s modernism.

Montage and mediation in the manifesto form

The first thing to note about the *Communist Manifesto* as a text is that
it is the syncretic product of a number of pre-existing, historically discrete
literary forms; each of which represents a separate compositional element,
the history of which may be traced through the *Manifesto*'s relations to
earlier texts and manuscript materials by Marx and Engels themselves.
To begin with, for example, one might attend to the text's origins in the
'question and answer' form of Engels' *Principles of Communism* (October
1847), which was a revised version of the catechism form of his own
earlier *Draft of a Communist Confession of Faith*, from June of the same
year – the written-up version of the draft programme discussed at the
First Congress of the Communist League. Comparison of the three documents reveals successive transformations of the catechism form as it is
progressively subordinated to, and integrated into, a narrative form.

The change was Engels' idea, as we know from his letter to Marx of 23–4 November 1847, as was the idea of calling the final version a 'manifesto';[13] although it is important to note that Marx was the sole author of the text of the *Manifesto* itself. The use of the word 'manifesto' seems to have been suggested by the re-publication that year of the French socialist Victor Considèrent's *Principles of Socialism* (orginally published in 1843) which was subtitled *Manifesto of the Democracy of the Nineteenth Century*.[14] However, while the basic meaning of the term 'manifesto' as a document which 'makes manifest', in the sense of making a public demonstration of something, was already established by this time – the first example appears to be Sylvain Maréchal's *Manifeste des Egaux*, 1796 – it is important to note that most of the main characteristics which are now taken to be distinctive of the manifesto as a literary form were more or less defined by the *Communist Manifesto* itself.[15]

The first version, Engels' *Draft of a Communist Confession of Faith* (June 1847) begins:

> Question 1: *Are you a Communist?*
> Answer: Yes.
> Question 2: *What is the aim of the Communists?*
> Answer: To organize society in such a way that every member of it can develop and use all his [/her] capacities and powers in complete freedom and without thereby infringing the basic conditions of society.
> Question 3: *How do you wish to achieve this aim?*
> Answer: By elimination of private property and its replacement by common property ...[16]

This is a suitable form for a secret society, an illegal organization – as the League of the Just had been, out of which the Communist League emerged – or a religious sect. It is a formal, repetitive, ritualized dialogue form.

In Engels' second version ('wretchedly worded' on account of being written in a 'tearing hurry', as he put it), four months later, this has become:

> Question 1: *What is Communism?*
> Answer: Communism is the doctrine of the conditions for the emancipation of the proletariat.
> Question 2: *What is the proletariat?*
> Answer: The proletariat is that class of society which ...[17]

The mode of address has been generalized and objectivized. The content of the dialogue is no longer focused on the existential dimension of being and acting, on becoming a communist – a confession of faith – but on the principles of the doctrine itself. We have moved from the cellar or attic into the schoolroom.

In the final version, the *Manifesto* itself, written by Marx in January 1848, after a brief period of collaboration with Engels the previous month, there is a dramatic shift of register into the famous Gothic narrative mode:

> A spectre is haunting Europe – the spectre of Communism. [Or, if you prefer, the most recent, anti-Derridean translation, returning to Helen McFarlene's original, 1850 rendition of the German verb, *umgehen in*: A spectre *stalks* the land of Europe.] All the powers of old Europe have entered into a holy alliance to exorcise this spectre: Pope and Czar, Metternich and Guizot, French radicals and German police spies. . . .

Or, if one takes Section One as the proper beginning, the shift of register is into a sweeping historical panorama:

> The history of all hitherto existing societies is the history of class struggles.
>
> Freeman and slave, patrican and plebian, lord and serf, guild-master and journeyman, in a word, oppressor and oppressed, stood in constant opposition to one another, carried on an uninterrupted, now hidden, now open fight, a fight that each time ended, either in a revolutionary re-constitution of society at large, or in the common ruin of the contending classes.

Only at the very end of Section Two, nearly two thirds of the way through the text as a whole, do we find the programmatic list of measures that the communists plan to undertake. This is another embedded form: the political programme.

By comparison, the *Draft of a Communist Confession of Faith* placed the demands of the movement up front, although it stated them only in the most general terms. Moreover, here, in the *Manifesto*, these demands are subordinated to a wider narrative, within which they are but a transitional moment, extending into a qualitatively different future, which climaxes with an account of what it is that 'we shall have' in place of the old bourgeois society: 'an association, in which the free development of each is the condition for the free development of all.' The temporal locus of the text is no longer the eternal present of secret society or schoolroom, but the contradictory historical present of capitalist societies, packed tight with the productive energies of human history and the accumulated memories of struggles between classes, bursting with the anticipation of a specific future (communism).

Yet the existential dimension of the earlier versions persists, not merely in the phenomenological force of the descriptions of the revolutionary temporality of capitalist societies (highlighted by Berman) and the degradation of labour within them (which he ignores), but in the intermittent eruption within the narrative of the 'we' and the 'you': the registration in direct speech of the displaced survival of the catechism, through which the contradictions of the historical process are given voice in rhetorical form. There is a subtle interweaving within the text of the *Manifesto* of what Benveniste distinguishes with his technical use of the terms 'narrative' and 'discourse': where *discourse* is a linguistic form marked by the temporal proximity of its objects to the present of its utterance, while *narrative* cultivates temporal distance and objectivity, through the preferential use of the third person, along with the aorist, imperfect and pluperfect tenses, avoiding the present, perfect and future.[18] This is in many ways a problematic distinction, theoretically, but it is useful here nonetheless, to register the shifts between verb tenses and modes of address within the *Manifesto*, through which the enormous weight of its narrative content (history as the history of modes of production and the conflicts between their constitutive social classes) is brought to bear on the point of the present of reading.

For example, Section Two of the *Manifesto* begins in the schoolmasterly, question-and-answer mode of Engels' *Principles of Communism* – 'In what relation do the Communists stand to the proletarians as a whole?' – but as the answer develops, voices proliferate. Objections interject ('Do you mean the property of the petty artisan and of the small peasant, a form of property that preceded the bourgeois form? . . . Or do you mean modern bourgeois property?'), multiply ('But does wage labour create any property for the labourer?') and are rebuffed ('Not a bit. It creates capital.'). The text becomes the site of an argument in the fullest sense of the word, as the reader is pulled back and forth between different standpoints, within the overall narrative flow.

Allied to this is the complex universality and singularity of the text's 'we'. Not only is the dialogical 'you' – 'You are horrified at our intending to do away with private property' – multiple and flexible, projecting the reader into the position of various objectors, but Marx also clearly exploits the fourth of the poets' rights ordered by the first of the Russian Futurist manifestos: namely, the right 'to stand on the rock of the word "we" amidst the sea of boos and outrage'.[19] This rock is only rarely inhabited these days; people fear the colonizing impulses it arouses. Yet Marx's 'we' is at once differential and cumulative. It is the authorial 'we' of the writer; the more inclusive 'we' of author and readers (the 'we' of 'as we have seen, above'); the specific and strongly distinguishing 'we' of 'we communists'; and finally, climactically, it is the universal 'we' of the 'we shall have', which is also the 'we' of *what* we shall have: namely, 'an association in which the free development of each [each 'I'] is the condition for the free development of all' – the 'we' of an *absolute* (one might say, a 'philosophical') universality via which the reader passes, almost without noticing, into the standpoint of a post-capitalist historical view; a 'we' through which we readers, in the present, are offered an oppositional political identity within the present, through identification with the *individuated* universality of a 'we' of the future: 'an association in which . . . each . . . for . . . all'.

Finally, one might mention the length of the text, the duration of reading and conceiving. The *Manifesto*'s combination of briefness (a mere fourteen thousand words), with breadth (human societies past and future), characteristic of the manifesto as a form, produces a vibrant imagism at the heart of the narrative, as vast swathes of historical experience are condensed into single images: 'all that is solid melts into air' (a translation, incidentally, that uses Shakespeare to improve considerably on Marx's German). The brevity of the text seals it up into an autonomous totality which figures history as a whole, producing an eschatological effect similar to that described by Walter Benjamin in his account of the production of 'now-time' out of the ruptural force of the dialectical image: the image at 'the now of recognisability', as he called it in his *Arcades Project*.[20]

It is surprising that Benjamin left us without a reading of the *Communist Manifesto*, without doubt the most 'Benjaminian' of Marx's texts, and, one might argue, the high point of the German Romantic influence on Marx (the essence of Romanticism, for Benjamin, lay in its messianism);[21] although there is an invocation of Marx's concept of revolution in the extraordinary final paragraph of his 'Surrealism' essay. Yet Benjamin did leave us an account of capitalist modernity as cultural meltdown – 'a vast process in which literary forms are being melted down'[22] – in his writings of the 1920s and 1930s. And he connected this meltdown, explicitly, to new experiences of time, associated with the interacting forces of commodification, technology and urbanism (one might add, migration); forces which gave rise to new media and forms of representation (photography, film, newspapers, advertisments) in relation to which the history of the manifesto form itself must be located. If, as Benjamin argued, Dadaism was an attempt to match the effects of film within the (technically obsolete) medium of painting,[23] so the *Manifesto* may be understood as an attempt to invent a new literary form of political communication appropriate to a period of mass politics on an international scale out of the obsolete form of the catechism and still vibrant Gothic tale. (A form in which ease of translation is an important feature of the directness of its style.) As Benjamin, once again, argued, 'One of the foremost tasks of art has always been the creation of a demand which could be fully satisfied only later'[24] – in this case, perhaps, by television.

The sense of an autonomous totality, produced by the sweeping historical overview of the first two sections of the *Manifesto* (Sections Three and Four are in many ways programmatic appendages), has all the radically temporalizing qualities associated by Benjamin with the timelessness of the dialectical image. We find a similar historiographical timelessness, or absolutization of narrative unity via a deregulation of the play of the opposition of 'narrative' to 'discourse', in Rancière's reading of Michelet as the historian of 'the absolute nominal phrase', which abolishes temporal markers in order to absolutize the meaning of the present.[25] The temporality of the *Manifesto* cannot be reduced to that of the absolute nominal phrase; it is far more internally complex than that. Yet a not-dissimilar effect is produced by its first two sections as a whole, by their imagistic force. They function much like a history painting, a triptych, in which images of past, present, and future coalesce as tensely interacting forms. In fact, one could argue, that this peculiar effect of *radical futurity via temporal suspension* is a feature of the manifesto form, in general, in which, as Tristan Tzara put it, one must 'organize prose into a form that is absolutely and irrefutably obvious'.[26] A manifesto being, on Tzara's definition: 'a communication made to the whole world, whose only pretension is the discovery of an instant cure for political, astronomical, artistic, parliamentary, agronomical and literary syphilis ... it is always right.'[27] This is the second connotation of 'making manifest' which is essential to the manifesto as form: something with a high degree of evidence. There is, first, the sense of *publicity*, in the political sense of being projected into a public space; second, a *high degree of evidence*. And finally, there is its connotation of demonstration, in the sense of being an *act* (rather than a mere representation): specifically, an *act of protest* against some existing state of affairs (as in the French sense of *manifestation*).

As Tzara saw so clearly, a manifesto is primarily a performance. (Tzara, incidentally, absolutizing this dimension, declared himself to be as against manifestos, 'in principle', as he was 'against principles'.)[28] The *Communist Manifesto* is distinguished by the way it offsets the arbitrariness of the literary absolutism inherent in the performative dimension of the manifesto form (demonstrated so brilliantly by Tzara) with historical argumentation woven throughout both its narrative and discursive modes. Ultimately, however, the force of this argument is dependent upon its integration into a structure of experience constructed by the manifesto as a form.

Marx drew on a multiplicity of received forms to forge the 'absolute obviousness' of the *Communist Manifesto*: the catechism, the historical narrative, the Gothic tale, the political programme – to which one might add the critique (the critique of political economy, condensed into the description of capitalism) and the literary review (of previous socialist and communist literature, in Section Three). Six different literary forms, at least, fused together within the framework of a seventh: the manifesto. The *Communist Manifesto* is a *montage*. It stages 'a rebirth of the epic out of the technique of montage'.[29] More specifically, it constructs a complex existential mediation of historical time through a syncretic combination of historically discrete literary forms, each of which retains an aspect of autonomy within the whole. It embodies a historical futurity of qualitative newness, independent of its penultimate narrative act (proletarian revolution), in the historical dimension of its cultural form. Add to this, the contextual dimension of its reception – the way in which meaning is produced as an articulation or reorganization of existing structures of experience – and one begins to get a sense of the extraordinary density of historical relations which underlie and animate the apparent simplicity of its appeal. None of this is registered in Berman's modernist reading; brilliant as it is in its one-dimensional way.

In fact, even the famous 'spectre' – or as Helen McFarlane translated *Gespenst*, the 'frightful hobgoblin' – is borrowed.[30] (Her translation in the *Red Republican* of November 1850 begins: 'A frightful hobgoblin stalks throughout Europe.') Doubly borrowed, in fact, since Marx's first paragraph appears to involve a reflective synthesis of an original passage and an already existing borrowing. To begin with, there is Lorenz von Stein's *Socialism and Communism in Present Day France* (1842), in which we find the reference to communism as 'an ominously threatening spectre [*drohenden Gespenst* – Stein's translator has "threatening nightmare", another possible rendering of *Gespenst*], in whose actuality no one wants to believe'. Then there is Wilhelm Schulz entry on 'Communism' in the *Staatslexicon* (1846), which turns this into: 'For a few years in Germany there is talk of Communism, and already it has become a threatening spectre [*drohenden Gespenst*] for those who fear it and with which others seek to create fear.'[31] The literary superiority of Marx's *Ein Gespenst geht um in Europa* – 'A spectre stalks the land of Europe', in Carver's recent translation – is clear, in its elegance and economy. As is the joint, political-theoretical, use to which the metaphor is put in the passage which follows, in which we are presented with the idea of replacing this 'nursery tale' (Moore) or, better perhaps, 'horror story' (Carver) with an account of how things actually stand, historically.

Contra Derrida – there is nothing *unheimliche* about Marx's spectre – since it doesn't come from the past, but, as a fearful, imaginary projection, from the future.[32] Marx is consequently able to accomplish a characteristic literary trick here, of transferring the rhetorical power of an image which he is actually setting out to 'demystify' onto the process of demystification itself. (The move from catechism to narrative was intended by Engels to signify the move away from a Fourier-type 'literary or utopian' socialism towards a 'scientific' approach. Engels' own *Draft of a Communist Confession of Faith* was deficient in this regard, since it retained significant elements from Moses Hess's *Communist Confession in Questions and Answers* of 1844, from which it partly derived.) This method of 'escaping literature by means of literature', as Andy Parker has succinctly described it,[33] achieves an almost sublime dialectical ambiguity in Marx's use of the manifesto form.

The dual, political-theoretical logic of this extraordinary transformation of catechism into narrative, and narrative into manifesto, draws attention to a further consequence of the montage-like principle of construction which lies beneath the synthetic unity of Marx's manifesto form: montage functions here as a principle, not only of sociality – the sociality embedded in the received forms – but also of *collectivity*, a collective political project. Since it is above all else the history of socialist literature – subjected to analytical critique in Section Three – which provides the materials for Marx's critical-synthetic act. None of the ideas in the *Manifesto* are new. It is a wholly synthetic, appropriative literary act. Its demand on the future, its 'we shall have' ('we shall have an association, in which the free development of each is the condition for the free development of all') is a universalized demand in the aesthetic-existential sense of that demand about which Kant writes in the *Critique of Judgment*: the 'strange' demand made by a reflective judgment of singularity which requires agreement from all.[34] It is a mistake to take this 'we shall have' for a prediction, in any scientific sense of the term. The *Manifesto* displays, in a practical form, a sophistication about historical temporality which is sadly lacking from Marx's methodological writings about history.

To sum up the argument against Berman: there is a complex plurality of times and forms of organization of experience at play in the literary form of the *Communist Manifesto* in addition to the revolutionary temporality of capital; forms of temporality which survive the demotion in the narrative historical role of its main character (the proletariat, purported agent of the new era); forms of futurity which construct the prospect of the qualitative historical novelty of a post-capitalist society out of the articulation of the contradictions of the existing social form. (As Wolfgang Haug put it: the book is governed by a 'grammar of contradiction'.)[35] Berman's Marx, on the other hand, is a one-dimensional modernist, in thrall to the disintegrative effects of time itself. Berman's reading of the *Manifesto* aims to 'give modernist art and thought a new solidity and invest its creations with an unsuspected resonance and depth'.[36] Yet it is the pure temporal modernism of the desire for the new, the new as an invariant, alone, which he uncovers; thereby robbing the *Manifesto* of its distinctive historical resonance and depth. For the *Manifesto* surely belongs to another modernism, to what Jeff Wall has called 'the dream of a modernism with social content', an 'openly socially critical modernist art',[37] in which formal innovation is a reflective but nonetheless *constructive* play with the culturally mediated aspects of social forms; a modernism for which form is the medium for the expression of the contradictions of historically specific social relations, within the horizon of their sublation. This dream continues to inspire a diverse array of cultural projects. It serves well as a description of Walter Benjamin's work. The idea that cultural forms are sites for the articulation of social contradictions is central to such a dream. I shall therefore end with some brief remarks about the absence from Berman's reading of the *Manifesto* of the contradictory social content underlying the temporality of capital; an absence which, read symptomatically, draws our attention to certain crucial weaknesses within the *Manifesto* itself.

Fantasy, utopianism, and 'sober sense'

Adorno once remarked that the problem with what he called the 'loathsome question' of 'what is living and what is dead' in the work of a particular thinker – the question of what in it has any meaning for the present – is that the converse inquiry is never made: namely, what is living in the present – what the present means – from the standpoint of that thinker's work.[38] Such a dialectical, historical but anti-historicist approach casts Berman's reading of Marx in a harsh light. For it is a remarkable feature of Berman's reading of the *Manifesto* that while it restricts itself to the horizon of capital (positing capital as the source of its utopian energy), it is nonetheless parasitic on a utopian vision that is integrally connected to Marx's discourse on communism, a discourse which Berman neglects. This is the sleight of hand that transfigures Marx's appreciation of the enormous, but relative, historical advance of capitalism into an *absolutization* of its productivity, independent of its status as a historical (and therefore, of necessity, a *passing)* social form. Berman transfers the 'absolutism' of the *Manifesto*'s theoretical and literay form wholly onto capital, yet, from the standpoint of the text's narrative structure, the (socially contradictory) productivity of capitalism appears as a historical advance only from the point of view of a *post*-capitalist future; a point of view that Berman's Marx can no longer sustain. In this respect (with regard to the temporal logic of the text), Berman's reading suffers from a fatal incoherence: it invests capital with a utopian charge which cannot, even theoretically, be redeemed. Hence its ultimate reduction of utopianism to *energetics*: 'the glory of modern energy and dynamism, the ravages of modern disintegration and nihilism', and 'the strange intimacy between them'. What Berman leaves out is any account of the social sources of the dynamism of capital, the revolutionary temporality of which he celebrates.

The reason this was possible lies within the *Manifesto* itself: in a series of systematic slippages and contradictions in its treatment of the relations between its four main ideas of *bourgeoisie, proletariat, communism* and *capital*. The *Manifesto*: 1) conflates the bourgeoisie with capital; while 2) placing the proletariat outside of capital (neglecting its existence as variable capital); thereby 3) enabling a conflation of the proletariat with communism; while 4) reducing capitalism to the logic of capital (neglecting its articulations with other, historically received social forms). As a result, its 'discursive' futurity is curtailed, subordinated by the proletariat's 'narrative' role. The dynamism that the *Manifesto* attributes to the bourgeoisie ('i.e. capital', as the English translation has it at one point) must actually be considered an effect of the dialectic of social classes, as structured, not only by the conditions of capital accumulation, but by the *totality* of social relations obtaining at any particular time. (Think of the importance of immigration to the history of capitalism, for example; not simply in the paradigm-case of the USA, but as a whole.) The power of capital to annihilate received social forms has turned out to be considerably less absolute – indeed, considerably less desirable from the standpoint of the accumulation of capital – than Marx supposed. This is one of the main things that the *Manifesto* draws our attention to today, via the failure of its imagined negation: the continuing vitality within the most advanced capitalist societies of supposedly 'pre-capitalist' social forms.

It is extraordinary that Berman should choose to absolutize the disintegrative, purely abstract temporal modernism of the *Manifesto*'s 'melting' vision – the elimination of every social bond other than 'naked self-interest' – at the very moment when a whole complex of non-economic (or at least, not immediately economic) social relations has come to the fore, politically, in advanced capitalist societies, including all those that the *Manifesto* would have capitalism dissolve (religion, occupational status, family, nation, age, sex), along with others (such as race and ethnicity) which it fails to mention. This is of enormous significance, not only because of what it tells us about the importance to capitalism of what the value-form would destroy (or at best, ignore) – what Balibar calls 'the binding agents of a historical collectivity of individuals', which are subject to a contradictory reintegration into the circuits of capital[39] – but also because of what it has to tell us about the constitutive role of fantasy in social and political processes. For despite Berman's selection of 'sober sense' as one of the most important features of the *Manifesto*'s celebration of capitalism – the compulsion of men and women to face 'their real conditions of life and their relations with their kind' – sober sense, in this specific sense of a theoretically adequate 'demystified' sense, is actually and understandably rather thin on the ground. It is more likely to be via a consideration of the ineliminability of fantasy and imagination from the constitution of social and political identities, and their relations to the 'real conditions of life', that the connections between *finitude*, *futurity*, and *social form* are to be understood.

The social forms that Marx would have capitalism destroy live on within it, transformed, as both points of identification and functioning relations, suffused with fantasy in ways which cannot be fully comprehended apart from their non-capitalistic dimensions. In fact, in the newly Gothic consciousness of the post-communist era, capitalist societies increasingly appear as peopled by the living dead of so-called 'pre-capitalist' forms. This is quite different from the living dead of capital itself, which was, for Marx – as money was for Hegel – a 'self-propelling life of the dead' (dead labour).[40] A future beyond capitalism is figured here, not least, in the concept of political community. Writing of the experience of history made possible by the technology of the photograph, Benjamin remarked that

> the beholder feels an irresistible urge to search ... for the tiny spark of contingency, of the Here and Now, with which reality has so to speak seared the subject, to find the inconspicuous spot where in the immediacy of that long forgotten moment the future subsists so eloquently that we, looking back, may rediscover it.[41]

Reading the *Communist Manifesto* today, one can find a number of such spots, not in those parts that are closest to us, but in those 'sparks of contingency' that now seem farthest away.

5

TIME AND THE ARTWORK

There is a generally accepted account of the relationship of memory to historical consciousness which runs, broadly speaking, something like this. 1) History has its ontological basis and historical origin in the unity of individual and collective memory, as registered in the form of the epic (the unity of the one and the many narratives) and the structure of tradition, as the mechanism for securing continuity between the generations. However, 2) historiography proper, the history of the 'historians', history in its modern disciplinary, world-historical sense, begins only with the fracturing of this unity, the multiplication of reminiscences, and the consequent need for the artificial, methodological construction of collective memory through exterior, documentary sources. This is a process dependent upon writing (for both its objects and means) which, in the West, was revolutionized by the invention of printing at the end of the Middle Ages. Thus, in Europe, the period from the fourteenth to the eighteenth century may be seen as simultaneously 'the long death agony of the art of memory' in its core psychic sense (as charted, most famously, by Francis Yates) and the pre-history of historical scholarship, based on the establishment of centralized archival depositories and the foundation of state-sponsored libraries and museums, alongside the existing ecclesiastical institutions.[1]

In the nineteenth century, in Europe, *the* century of history *par excellence*, such scholarship was distinguished by three main features: i) an aspiration to *objectivism* in its methodologies (Ranke's past 'the way it really was' or Michelet's 'integral resurrection of the past'); ii) a primarily *national* and *statist* focus of interest; and iii) a belief in the unitary character of its ultimate object: History with a capital 'H', the history of humanity, *history as a whole* – whether this belief be residually theological or newly materialist in kind. However, while the narratives that were built upon such scholarship could claim a new epistemological (though not necessarily political) objectivism, they were of necessity distanced from the 'living' memories at work in the everyday practices of different social groups. As a result, the ontology of collective memory was transformed. Cut loose from its moorings in psychic and generational continuities with the past, by becoming properly 'historical', collective memory migrated from social practice into independent representational forms (historical texts), from whence it was reimported into everyday life, in the service of a variety of political projects, in the distinctively modern form of what have become known as 'invented traditions'.[2] Historical consciousness, in the strict sense, is thus 'memory' in an analogical sense only. Its logic is that of *construction*, rather than *recollection*, in a Platonic or even a Hegelian sense.

More recently, 3) technical developments in the means of representation have led to further extensions in the metaphorical scope of the idea of memory. From photography and sound recording to the computer, with its still growing capacity for massive quantitative expansions in data storage and retrieval, a variety of means of representation have come to 'embody' the past with sufficient indexicality to be considered to 'be' (or in the specific case of computers, to have) 'memories'. In the last fifty years, the documentary basis of historical research has been transformed, both quantitively and qualitatively, creating new problems for historiography. Meanwhile, the analogical objectivization of memory has gone a stage further, passing over into the biological sciences, where genetic codes are now routinely conceived as 'memories for heredity'. As a result, objects of memory are increasingly understood in cybernetic terms as embodiments of ontologically discrete forms of 'information', existing independently of the uses to which they might be put in either the present or future. 'Memory' has been alienated from its communicative function in the constitution of social identities, becoming autonomous and disembodied.

We live in a culture characterized simultaneously by an abundance of historical representations and a scarcity of historical consciousness, in the traditional sense of a form of experience linking the three phenomenological dimensions of temporal experience (past, present, and future) in a coherent, though not necessarily seamless, collective and transgenerational manner. This *de-temporalizing* precedence of a binary and merely combinatory conception of information over narrative meaning (from the standpoint of which all narrative increasingly appears not only 'unscientific' but mythic) may be considered a further, electronically-driven, stage of what, in the 1930s, Walter Benjamin understood as the 'crisis of experience' precipitated by the interruptive time-consciousness of modernity in its myriad social forms: in particular, for Benjamin, the 'exact repetition' of machino-facture, the 'eternalization' of novelty in the temporal logic of fashion, the daily novelties of the newspaper, the instantaneous 'shock' effects of the crowd and of warfare in an age of technology, the accelerated and unpredictable temporality of run-away inflation, the disjunctive structure of montage in film, and above all, the abstraction from lived relations of usefulness dictated by the logic of exchange-value and the commodity-form.[3] This is a list to which can now be added the familiar effects of subsequent electronic audio and visual media, and transport and communications technologies: the remote control 'zapping' of video and TV channels, the continuous automatic imaging of surveillance monitors, the compositional logic of word-processing, the cacophany of muzaks in public spaces, jet-lag, bombardment by e-mail, and the rest. In sum, a temporal culture of instantaneity and speed.

This so-called 'crisis of experience' is a crisis of historical experience, a crisis in the definition of 'experience' (*Erfahrung*) as being, of necessity, 'historical'. It takes the form of a de-historization of lived relations (their isolation from large-scale narrative meanings and, in particular, from a collective future) and, in place of historical temporality, what Benjamin saw as an aestheticization of cultural forms. *Aestheticization* and *instantaneity* are linked together here as elements of a re-naturalization of experience: the technological exploitation of a crudely corporeal functionality for merely reactive or compensatory forms of psychic gratification. The famous fascist 'aestheticization of politics' in Benjamin's 'Work of Art' essay is but one aspect of this more general commodity-led, de-historizing aestheticization of cultural form that is the central theme of Benjamin's phenomenology of modernity.[4] Aestheticization and de-historization are two sides of the same coin. More recent accounts of *de-realization*, *hyper-reality* and the *speed-image* add little to this picture, beyond a technical updating and a more extreme rhetorical gloss. The issue is not computerization as such, but a culture of instantaneity in all of its forms. These accounts do, however, subtract something crucial from Benjamin's version: namely, the urgent possibility of an oppositional, *re-historizing*, refiguring of temporal forms. For Benjamin, the temporality of modernity promotes a forgetting of history which – itself historical – can and *should be* contested from within.

Now, there are good philosophical as well as sociological reasons for contesting the absolutism of Benjamin's opposition of modernity to tradition, montage to narrative, image to story; and hence for doubting the apocalyptical tone of his account of the 'crisis' – reasons to do with the existential structure of temporalization and the transcendental status of narrativity, as argued, for example, by Ricoeur in his monumental *Time and Narrative*. They constitute the philosophical presuppositions of what follows.[5] Even more, should we doubt the latest, more fully ontologized, self-consciously excessive variants (Baudrillard and Virilio). Nonetheless, a variety of factors indicate that the crisis in the historical dimension of experience which so preoccupied Benjamin – and which he also found at the heart of historical study, in the blank chronologism of the time-consciousness of historicism, as acutely as elsewhere – not only continues but has intensified; not merely despite, but precisely *via* the forms of historical representation that predominate in advanced capitalist societies today: both at the level of 'lived experience' and within historiography. In the first case, these forms are still predominantly those of commodity consumption (commercially exploiting historical representation in the service of 'leisure' – what in Britain is called the 'heritage industry') and a reductively instrumental politics which feeds the perceived need for substantial social identities with ever more simplified images of the past, in a reactive restoration of the temporal structure of myth, which is indifferent to the complexities of actual social histories and utilizes the mechanisms of abstraction of commodity culture itself. The dimension of historical experience most profoundly affected (and effaced) by these forms is that of our relation to the future.

Ironically, this problem has been deepened, rather than challenged, by the democratization of historical discourses, which has underlaid the decline in the reputation of unitary, teleological models of history among professional historians since the 1960s and opened up a vast array of new historiographic sources.[6] For the intellectual and political tide that turned against the (state-inflected) paradigm of a totalizing or unified history, in favour of a democratic multiplicity of collective memories – returning history to its existential origins in memory – bases itself firmly in the *presently defined* realities of specific, differentially constituted social groups, as its point of orientation towards the past. Thus, the so-called 'new' (post-Foucauldian) history, with its discursive revolution in the concept of the archive and its rejection of the three main features of the nineteenth-century model (above), turns on what Le Goff identifies as the twin epistemological axes of 'contemporary problematics . . . retrospective procedures'.[7] It is as if Michelet's famous assertion that 'History is first of all geography' had come back to haunt him. The newly differential social geography destroys the aspiration to an integral past. The practical basis of historical consciousness in the present realities of specific social subjects is restored (and with it, to a certain extent, the idea of history as memory), but only at the cost of a relativization of its epistemic claims and social function which problematizes the concept of democracy itself. One does not have to agree with declarations of a 'perpetual present' or 'post-historical' age to recognize within the new history itself the signs of another de-historization, resistant to the spatial generalization of the totalizing structure of temporalization into an overall historical view, however fallible, heuristic, and projective its claims on a common humanity might be.

Where, and how, do contemporary art and art criticism fit into this picture of de-historization, de-temporalization and reactive mythologization? The link is aestheticization. The issue is the relationship between the historical and the aesthetic in what, following Adorno, I shall call 'artistic experience' (*künstlerischen Erfahrung*) – the experience of the artwork – something which is more often than not reductively *mis*described as 'aesthetic experience'. I shall restrict my remarks in this chapter to the contradictory relationship to historical time established by the role of

81

the aesthetic in Greenberg's modernist criticism, and the possibility of an alternative account of the time of artworks as fields for the temporalization of history, which emphasizes their differential historical temporality.

Modernism, criticism, de-historization

It is a virtue of Greenberg's model of modernism that, in its origins at least, in the late 1930s and early 1940s, it attempted to base itself on a mode of historicality immanent to the productive logic of the art of the time. Thus, rather than following art history in its adoption of the time-consciousness of nineteenth-century historicism, its notion of modernism as self-criticism operated with a genuinely 'tensed' conception of historical time centred on the historical present of the enunciative act (in this case, the production of the artwork) and its relations of negation to past events (previous artworks).[8] In Benveniste's terms, it was first of all 'discourse' and only secondarily 'narrative'.[9] However, it was necessarily narrative as well, and it is from the increasing reification of this narrative element (a progressivist narrative of medium-specific aestheticization or 'purification'), with a fixed point of origin, that its problems derive. For there is a paradoxical temporal doubling inherent in the conceptual structure of the 'modern' that Greenberg's criticism found increasingly hard to negotiate.

This doubling derives from the fact that 'modernity' functions simultaneously as both a signifier of a period, within the terms of an objective, typological, chronological historiography, and a self-referential, performative designation of the (changing) time of its utterance, the time of the analysis itself. As I have argued elsewhere, in this latter, productive respect, it is 'the product, in the instance of each utterance, of an act of historical self-definition through differentiation, identification and projection, which transcends the order of chronology in the construction of a meaningful present'.[10] As the name of the historical present, the present as history, all definitions of modernity (including artistic modernity) are at once *iterative* and inherently *political*. They construct specific positions of historical enunciation and address, provoking what Homi Bhabha has described as 'a continual questioning of the conditions of existence; making problematic ... [their] own discourse not simply as "ideas" but as the position and status of the locus of social utterance'.[11] Each repetition of the sign of modernity is different. Yet, by virtue of a common temporal structure, each repetition raises the question of its relations of other modernities; relations which are at once historical and projective, referential and constructed. However, such semantic fluidity (centred in the 'now' of each new production) runs counter to the narrative fixation of 'periods' for which empirical attributes must be abstracted from each specific present as a basis for typological generalization.

In Greenberg, as we know, the basis for such generalization was the reduction of artworks to the aesthetic dimensions of their traditionally (that is, retrospectively) defined media. For the visual arts, this meant the tendential *elimination* of the temporal dimension of aesthetic experience.[12] There are thus at least three different temporalities at play in Greenberg's account of the modernist work: 1) the productive, interruptive temporality of 'the new', through which each work defines its own historical present via its difference from the works of the past; 2) the idealized 'no-time' of aesthetic appreciation, through which the work presents itself as a purely spatial phenomenon inhabiting a kind of eternity (the classical); 3) holding the contradiction between 1) and 2) together, the narrative temporality of progressivism, with its regulation of interruption as series, on the basis of an underlying directional chronologism. Unfairly perhaps, we might call this the time of art history. This is the point at which Greenberg's art criticism approaches the art history of the traditional art historian.

The first (avant-garde) form is radically temporalizing and historizing. Every work is a definition of the present in the name of the future. It is the function of a modernist criticism 'to speak the words of the future in the present'.[13] The second and third are both de-historizing, although in different ways. The second ('aesthetic') temporality is that of a paradoxical de-temporalization, an evacuation of temporality from the object. Modelled on a certain Kantian transcendentalism, it has affinities with – but should be rigorously distinguished from – the interruptive no-time of the instant. It is linked by Greenberg to 'autonomy', which he understands narrowly as self-referentiality. The third (narrative) temporality is de-historizing to the extent that it performs a historicist effacement of futurity. In each of the latter two cases, time appears as a mere external medium, external to the 'working' of the work.

The suppressed contradiction between the historical and the (idealized) 'aesthetic' aspects of this approach manifests itself as soon as artistic production strays beyond the parameters of the historical moment defining the aesthetic conception of the work. This was already happening to Greenberg by the mid-1950s in the USA (the time of his greatest critical purchase on contemporary art), in the work of Rauschenberg and Johns, and it became increasingly (polemically) explicit in the context of the Pop, Minimalist, and Conceptual work of the 1960s.[14] That is to say, Greenberg's modernism was rendered anachronistic as soon as historical experiences imposed themselves at the level of artistic form which, by virtue of their claim on the present, could no longer be ignored. How, though, can we construe the artwork in a fully historical manner without neglecting or annihilating the constitutive significance of its specifically aesthetic dimension?

The key lies in the unity of art criticism and art history; although not the art history of the traditional art historian. The key lies in the art history of the art critic: the iterative social constitution of the work through the field of historical judgment, as embodied in the totality of critical practices that make up the art institution. For the claim made by the work as 'art' is not itself 'aesthetic' as such. Rather, it is a claim made *via* the aesthetic which cannot be made any other way. Art is historical insofar as it *signifies*: re-presents experience sensuously as meaning. Art transcends aesthetics as soon as we make the move from sensibility to *meaning* – a move which is never completed, but constantly doubles back upon itself, renewing meaning through sensuousness, fracturing meaning against sensuousness. Art becomes historical to the extent to which this meaning is the object of autonomous judgments of artistic truth. However, it is the aesthetic itself which, through its *figuring* of autonomy, makes judgments about art's (historical) truth possible.

Thus while, on the one hand, registering the autonomy of artistic experience from immediate practical interest, the aesthetic dimension is *idealizing* and *de-temporalizing*; on the other hand, it thereby projects the work into a domain of judgment, which is of necessity *conceptual*, *comparative* and *historical* in kind. The de-temporalizing function of the aesthetic may thus be read as the basis for a *re*-historization of experience, through artistic judgment. For art to function as the form of historical experience that it (potentially) is, however, requires a critical discourse that the objectivizing narrative of Greenberg's hegemonic modernism fails to provide. Less still, however, is it provided by its self-declaredly 'postmodern', 'post-historical' successors, since they forego the potentiality of the crisis in the aesthetic definition of the artwork brought about by Pop, Minimalism and Conceptualism, in favour of a dissolution of the concept of the artwork altogether.[15]

All three of these art movements reflect upon different aspects of the paradoxical process of the de-temporalization of memory as 'information': the de-temporalizing abstraction of the distribution-image of the commodity-form (Pop); of a pure spatial objectivization (Minimalism); and of ideation (Conceptualism), respectively. In this respect, at least, Conceptual art was less an art 'after philosophy' – for all its philosophical self-consciousness, it was hardly the first art-form to interrogate the concept of art – than an art 'after information'. (Two of the landmark exhibitions in New York in 1970 were entitled 'Information' and 'Software', at the Museum of Modern Art and the Jewish Museum, respectively.) Conceptual art used the ironic deployment of an alienated ontology of 'language' to highlight the lack of autonomy of visual form. Yet it remained naive about both its own dependence upon the aesthetic dimension and the de-temporalizing consequences of its purely ideational self- consciousness. Similar points apply to the newer, technologically-driven performance art of Stellark and Orlan which, for all its radicalism, struggles to rise above the level of a mere cultural symptomology. For if contemporary art is to remain a form of historical experience, it must continue to pass through the de-temporalizing form of the aesthetic on its way to a re-historization of everyday life.

6

CONCEPTUAL ART AND/AS PHILOSOPHY

It is difficult to bungle a good idea.

Sol LeWitt

Nothing marks the gulf separating the Conceptual art of the late 1960s and early 1970s from its post- and neo-Conceptual progeny of today more strikingly than their respective relations to philosophy. Indeed, one might be tempted to claim that it is in the intimacy of its relationship to philosophy – an intimacy at times verging on complete identification – that the specificity of Conceptual art resides, were its formation not so multiple and complex, despite its relatively brief life, as to refuse any such straightforward definition. Philosophy has been deployed too often as a weapon in the wars between Conceptual artists to be used unproblematically either as part of the criteria for the conceptuality of a work or as a neutral medium for debate about it. In this respect, even to raise the question of the relationship of Conceptual art to philosophy as an issue through which to re-examine the idea of Conceptual art is already to court the danger of situating oneself on one particular side of a series of factional divides. Yet it is precisely here, I shall argue, in its divisive, polemical role within the Conceptual art community that the importance of philosophy for Conceptual art lies, including its less explicitly or directly philosophical manifestations.

The very formulation of the problem is peculiar. For what does it mean to specify or delimit a particular kind of art with reference to its determination by another cultural field? Not a particular position within that field, it would seem – a particular philosophy – let alone a particular philosophy of *art*, but philosophy itself, philosophy as such. What does 'philosophy' stand for here? Pure conceptuality, pure thought, pure reason, perhaps? Or the historically developed and institutionally structured space of philosophical positions and possibilities which make up the professional *field of philosophical production*, at any particular time, in any particular place, in Bourdieu's sociological sense of the term?[1] Certainly, there were (and still are) Conceptual artists with highly invested, if deeply ambivalent, relationships to the discourses of professional philosophy; while others remained oblivious to its charms. Yet either way, whether the idea of philosophy is broadly or narrowly construed, the determination of a mode of artistic production by a philosophical form would seem to place it in opposition, in principle, to the established conception of 'art' in its modern European sense as *sensuous particularity* or *aesthetic*, bugbear of the Western philosophical imagination since Plato.[2]

This is, of course, the point: the shock, the scandal, the attractiveness and the enduring radicalism of the idea. Conceptual art is not just another particular kind of art, in the sense of a further specification of an existing genus, but an attempt at a fundamental redefinition of art as such, a transformation of its genus: a transformation in the relationship of sensuousness to conceptuality within the ontology of the artwork which challenges its definition as the object of a specifically 'aesthetic' (that is, 'non-conceptual') or quintessentially 'visual' experience. Conceptual art was an attack on the art object as the site of a look. That Conceptual art appears now as one particular kind of art among others is testimony to the fact that its moment has passed, that its challenge has faded. That a large amount of the art amidst which it appears, appears differently to the way in which art appeared before Conceptual art, attests to its enduring affect. Moreover, that both the intension (meaning) and the extension (reference) of the term 'Conceptual art' remain so hotly disputed registers the fact that there is unfinished business here to conduct.[3] Part of this business concerns the precise sense in which Conceptual art might be said to be a specifically 'philosophical' art; indeed, in which *all* art, after Duchamp (or at least, after the renewed reception of Duchamp in the 1960s; 'Duchamp' is largely a retrospective effect of the 1960s), might be said to be distinctively 'philosophical' in nature.[4]

It is important, in this respect, to distinguish two different levels at which disputes about the relationship between Conceptual art and philosophy have been conducted: 1) a level at which those advocating an expansive, empirically diverse and historically inclusive use of the term 'Conceptual art' confront the champions of narrower, analytically more restricted, and explicitly 'philosophical' definitions; and 2) a lower – and often more heated – level at which the latter dispute among themselves about the precise character of such definitions and the meaning and implications of their related practices and inquiries. I shall refer to those who advocate an expansive, empirically diverse and historically inclusive use of the term 'Conceptual art' (such as Sol LeWitt) as *inclusive* or *weak* Conceptualists. I shall call those championing more restricted, analytically focused and explicitly philosophical definitions (such as Kosuth and the British group Art & Language) *exclusive* or *strong* Conceptualists.

Exclusive or strong Conceptualists have tended to hog the critical limelight, for two reasons: first, because of the categorial extremism of their positions (they push hardest against the limits of the established notion of art); second, because of the affinity of their artistic practices to the practice of criticism. The relationship between Conceptual art and philosophical discourse in the USA and Britain in the late 1960s and early 1970s was dynamic, wild and not infrequently paradoxical. That there was a relationship at all was the result of changes in the relations between art practice and art criticism which took place in the first half of the 1960s, prior to the emergence of Conceptual art, strictly speaking, as a self-conscious form. On the one hand, these changes were an integral part of the development (and crisis) of Greenbergian modernist criticism in its interaction with new – especially 'Minimalist' – work. On the other hand, they were an effect of broader changes in educational provision, the social function of the arts, and politics in advanced capitalist societies. They involved both an increasing emphasis within art-critical discourse upon definitional questions about the essential nature or legitimate form of artworks, and a growing willingness on the part of artists themselves to engage in such discourse, both as a productive resource for practice and as a means of maintaining control over the representation of their projects within the artworld. This quickly led to an erosion of the division of labour between critic and artist, which had emerged in Europe during the second half of the nineteenth century and had been consolidated into the professional practices of the US artworld in the period immediately following the Second World War. Its most radical effect was an expansion in the notion of art practice (and hence, the art work) to include – at its limit – the products of all of the artist's art-related activities.

The crisis of Greenbergian criticism (essentially a crisis in its medium-based conception of the artwork, its 'specific' modernism) thus simultaneously registered a crisis in the ontology of the artwork and established the conditions for the resolution of this crisis through the renovation of the romantic ideology of artistic intentionality in a radically new, critical-discursive guise. Philosophy was *the means* for this usurpation of critical power by a new generation of artists: the means by which they could simultaneously address the crisis of the ontology of the artwork (through an art-definitional conception of their practice) and achieve social control over the meaning of their work. As such, Conceptual art represents a radical attempt to realign two hitherto independent domains of the cultural field: the field of artistic production and the field of philosophical production. More specifically, it involved an attempt directly to transfer the *cultural authority* of the latter into the former, thereby both bypassing and trumping existing forms of art-critical discourses. In this respect, Conceptual art is a classical example of strategic position-taking within a regional domain of the cultural field ('art'), aimed at a redistribution of the positions constituting that domain as a relational structure of possible actions.[5]

The discursive conditions for this transference of cultural authority were established by Greenberg, in the idea of modernist art as a self-critical art which explores the definition of its medium. (This notion of self-criticism was already an explicitly philosophical idea, borrowed directly from Kant's critique of reason.) The social conditions lay in the expansion and transformation of art education during the 1960s, in a context of growing cultural and political radicalism. The generation of New York artists who came to prominence in the 1960s were the first group of artists to have attended university. Their reaction against the anti-intellectualism of the prevailing ideology of the artworld – which was at once a reaction against its social conservatism – was profound. The result was a double-coding of 'philosophy' across the two cultural fields – artistic and phil-osophical – which introduced a constitutive ambiguity into the position of philosophy within the artistic field itself. Thus, on the one hand, phil-osophy functions within the artistic field as a specific form of artistic or critical material or productive resource for a practice the logic of which is supposedly autonomous or immanently artistic. On the other hand, philosophy retains its own immanent criteria of intellectual adequacy as itself a relatively autonomous cultural practice. That is, one may judge the adequacy of the philosophical ideas in play in the artworld both 'strictly philosophically' and from the standpoint of their contribution to the transformation of artistic practices. The idea of Conceptual art, in the exclusive or strong sense, is the *regulative fantasy* that these two sets of criteria might become one. The practice of strong Conceptualism was the experimental investigation – the concrete elaboration through practice – of the constitutive ambiguity produced by this founding double-coding.

Only a certain kind of philosophy could have played this role: namely, an analytical philosophy which combined the classical cultural authority of philosophy, in the updated guise of a philosophical scientism (logico-linguistic analysis), with a purely second-order or meta-critical conception of its epistemological status. For only a meta-critical conception of phil-osophy allows for the *re-coding* of 'art' as 'philosophy' while leaving its artistic status intact; rather than, like Hegel (or Danto), presenting them as competing modes of representation, and hence conceiving of Conceptual art as the *end of art*, to the precise extent to which it involves art becoming philosophical.[6] 'Art after philosophy', in Kosuth's sense, is very different from 'art after the end of art' in Danto's, despite their apparent similar-ities. The scientistic self-image of such philosophy was a crucial factor in the cultural logic of the exchange. For Anglo-American analytical phil-osophy offered a radically different art-educational ideal, and with it, a new image of the artist as an intellectually rigorous creator; more intellectual, in fact, than the increasingly beleaguered critic who would aspire to pass judgement on the meaning of the work. Such an image was at once a challenge to the prevailing image of the artist as a creative individual and cultural outsider and the means for its reconstruction on newly intellectual grounds. For the romantic sense of outsider-dom could be displaced onto the otherness of philosophy to the prevailing artworld and art-educational culture, allowing for the reproduction of certain characteristically 'artistic' (and often distinctively gendered) traits in the medium of their negation of the established form. In the British context, this dynamic was subsequently reinforced by the intellectual and political culture of Marxism, within which the image of the artist-as-political-activist was overlaid upon that of the artist-as-philosospher to produce a new (and often self-righteous) version of the artist-as-outsider. The artist-as-outsider became the artist-outside-of-'art'.

The structure of this rich and contradictory relationship between an art calling itself 'Conceptual' and philosophical discourse in the USA and Britain in the late 1960s and early 1970s may be traced, schematically, through the escalating philosophical investments of three canonic figures – Sol LeWitt, Joseph Kosuth and the British group Art & Language. This procedure should not be taken to imply that these figures are the most important Conceptual artists of their day; or that their work is in some way archetypical of Conceptual art more generally. It is not. Rather, these are the figures in whose work the question of the relationship of Conceptual art to *philosophy* stands out in sharpest relief. Any more comprehensive elaboration of the notion of Conceptual art will need to situate this aspect of its history in relation to a much wider set of determinations.[7] Which is not say that such an elaboration might not itself be, ultimately, philosophical in form. LeWitt, Kosuth and Art & Language represent three degrees of investment of Conceptual art in 'philosophy'. A brief comparison of the form and effects of these investments will lead us towards a provisional judgement on the significance of philosophy for the idea of Conceptual art.

Philosophy degree zero: Sol LeWitt

As a movement, Conceptual art is conveniently dated from the publication of Sol LeWitt's 'Paragraphs on Conceptual Art' in *Artforum* in the summer of 1967. LeWitt's essay was not the first to identify a particular kind of art as distinctively conceptual: an art in which 'the idea or concept is the most important part of the work'.[8] The Fluxus artist Henry Flynt had written about concept art – 'of which the material is *concepts* as the material of e.g. music is sound' – several years previously, in 1961.[9] Indeed, in George Maciunas's 'Genealogical Chart of Fluxus' (1968), Flynt is credited with formulating the idea as early as 1954. However, it was only with LeWitt's 'Paragraphs' that the idea achieved an extended critical thematization, and it was via LeWitt's 'Paragraphs' that it took hold in the US artworld as a unifying framework for the self-understanding of an emergent body of work. One reason for this was the breadth and inclusivity of LeWitt's construction of the category, in contrast to the proliferation of more restricted, lower-level critical terms, such as 'Minimalism' (drived from 'Minimal art', coined by Richard Wolheim in 1965), 'primary structures, reductive, rejective, cool, and mini-art', all of which LeWitt explicitly rejected as 'part of the secret language that art critics use when communicating with each other through the medium of art magazines'.[10] LeWitt's theorization is an exemplary defence of the standpoint of the artist against the critic, within the medium of criticism.

However, if LeWitt's essay marks the beginning of Conceptual art as a movement – however variegated and diffuse – it nonetheless reflects on the structure of an existing set of practices, which had previously been understood in a variety of alternative ways. (LeWitt is still predominantly categorized as a Minimalist, in fact.) In this respect, it is a transitional text and LeWitt is a transitional figure. 'Paragraphs on Conceptual Art' is a distillation of the immanent logic of an object-producing, though not object-based, practice which evolved, primarily, through the exploration of the effects of self-regulating series and systems of rules for decision-making about the production of objects out of pre-formed materials. As Robert Morris put it: 'Permuted, progressive, symmetrical organisations have a dualistic character in relation to the matter they distribute ... [They] separate ... from what is physical by making relationships them-selves *another order of facts*.'[11] For Morris, who retained a Greenbergian notion of truth to materials, this was problematic. For LeWitt, on the other hand, art was a privileged means of access to this other order of facts, which cannot be accessed directly in the same way. This explains the limited role attributed by the text to philosophy:

> Conceptual art doesn't really have much to do with mathematics, philosophy or any other mental discipline ... The philosophy of the work is implicit in the work and is not an illustration of any system of philosophy.[12]

Nor was LeWitt's Conceptualism linguistic in orientation. Flynt had argued that '[S]ince *concepts* are closely bound up with language, concept art is a kind of art of which the material is language.'[13] But LeWitt's art-ideas were as much *numerical* as linguistic. He would thus maintain the inde-pendently critical, rather than artistic, status of his analysis of Conceptual art, despite his famous insistence that 'The idea itself, even if not made visual, is as much a work of art as any finished product'.[14] 'These sentences comment on art', his later 'Sentences on Conceptual Art' (1969) concludes, 'but are not art.'[15] The idea, here, is the idea *of* a work of art; not a second-order idea *about* what a work of art is. The latter is criticism which, though it may contribute to the production of an art idea, is not one itself, as such. Insofar as there is philosophy in LeWitt, then, it is in his art and his criticism in qualitatively distinct forms.

Still, despite its origins in his own artistic practice, the idea of Conceptual art outlined in 'Paragraphs' had implications far beyond anything LeWitt was himself producing as art at the time. 'Conceptual' in comparison to certain other superficially similar works also often labelled 'Minimalist' (by Morris, for example), LeWitt's art appears as no more than 'proto-Conceptual' when set beside later, more single-mindedly conceptual work. One reason for this is that despite his gestures in the direction of a purely ideational interpretation of the artwork, LeWitt is actually ambivalent about objecthood. On the one hand, while declaring the look of a work to be its least important feature, and thereby downgrading its physicality in relation to its idea, the essay nonethless continues to treat the work's physical reality as a condition of its existence: 'It is the process of conception *and realization* with which the artist is concerned.' On the other hand, the remark that 'The idea itself, even if not made visual, is as much a work of art as any finished product' suggests that the physical reality of the work is not merely unimportant, but optional. But this is misleading, for LeWitt continues: 'All intervening steps – scribbles, sketches, drawing, failed work, models, studies, thoughts, conversations – are of interest. Those that show the thought process of the artist are sometimes more interesting than the final product.'[16]

What this reveals is that LeWitt is not really thinking ontologically about art's objecthood here at all; even if we consider the object intentionalistically, as an idea. Rather, more simply, he is concerned to valorize the intellectual element of the process of its production, which he associates, psychologistically, with the workings of the artist's mind. What looks like an exclusively *ideational* redefinition of the object, in conflict with the recognition that it requires some physical presence, is actually, more restrictively (and also, perhaps, more materialistically), a *psychological* one: 'A work of art may be understood as a conductor from the artist's mind to the viewer's.' LeWitt's proto-Conceptualist Minimalism is thus both ontologically dualistic (idea and object inhabit different realms) and a variant of realism in its understanding of ideas as mental events. This explains his distance from the predominantly anti-psychologistic forms of logico-linguistic analysis which would preoccupy later Conceptualists. Conceptual art, for LeWitt, is not theoretical but 'intuitive' – for all the apparent formalism of the ideas behind his own work. It is for this reason that he insists upon the 'mystical' rather than the 'rationalistic' character of such art, describing it as constituted by 'illogical judgements'.[17] Thus, while LeWitt may have pushed modernist reduction one stage further than Judd (from reduction to 'medium' to reduction to 'objecthood' to reduction to 'idea'), his psychological realism forbids the strictly conceptual reading of 'art as idea' which his 'Paragraphs' nonetheless inevitably evokes. It is thus not surprising that LeWitt would soon be challenged by a more exclusive, more formally philosophical, type of Conceptualism laying claim to the idea of 'art as idea' as its own.

It would be a mistake, though, to distinguish LeWitt from these later Conceptualists on the basis of the philosophical resources they deployed, alone. Adrian Piper, a staunch defender of an inclusive LeWittian Conceptualism, not only went on to study analytical philosophy, but became a professional philosopher, while continuing her career as an artist. However, she did not thereby become what I am calling a strong or exclusive Conceptualist. For while she used (and continues to use) her philosophical work in her art – often making work directly about her philosophical reflections – her philosophical interests are not in the concept of art itself, but in the broader metaphysical notions of space, time, and selfhood, the experience of which her art explores. (Initially, this was in a formal LeWittian manner; subsequently, in more social and political contexts, characterized by her interests in feminism and the politics of race.) For this LeWittian strand of Conceptualism, it is the *infinite plurality of media* that the idea of Conceptual art opens up which is the point, not the exploration of that idea itself, directly, as art. As Piper puts it: 'If we have to be concerned with one particular concept to be a conceptualist, something's gone badly wrong!'[18] LeWitt never considers the relationship between the ideational and physical aspects of the object, ontologically, in its specific character as 'art'. Indeed, the concept of art, as such, in its generality, plays little role in his thought. The distinctive feature of Kosuth's brand of analytical or strong Conceptualism, on the other hand, is its exclusive focus on the concept of art: its *reductively art-definitional* or *definitively philosophical* conception of art practice. It is at this point that a quite general engagement with art as a practice of manifest ideas (and hence only a very broad alignment of art with philosophy, as a discipline of conceptual ideality, like mathematics) is transformed into a particular engagement between modernist criticism (with its concern for the self-critical dimension of art as an autonomous practice) and a determinate state of the Anglo-American philosophical field.

First-degree philosophy: Joseph Kosuth

LeWitt's essay established the discursive conditions for Kosuth's formulation of his own ideas about Conceptual art, but these owe more to Duchamp and Reinhard than to LeWitt himself. They owe most of all to A.J. Ayer. Kosuth's Conceptualism takes up the functionalism of Duchamp's meta-artistic interventions and, discarding their residual anti-art negativity, reinterprets them in terms of a new linguistic positivism. It thereby extends the 'linguistic turn' characteristic of post-war Anglo-American philosophy into the field of artistic production in an ostensibly rigorous manner.

Being an artist now means to question the nature of art ... The function of art as a question, was first raised by Marcel Duchamp ... The event that made conceivable the realization that it was possible to 'speak another language' and still make sense in art was Marcel Duchamp's first unassisted readymade. With the unassisted readymade, art changed its focus from the form of the language to what was being said. Which means that it changed the nature of art from a question of morphology to a question of function. This change – one from 'appearance' to 'conception' – was the beginning of 'modern' art and the beginning of 'conceptual' art. All art (after Duchamp) is conceptual (in nature) because art only exists conceptually ... Artists question the nature of art by presenting new propositions as to art's nature.[19]

So runs the famous passage in 'Art After Philosophy', the serial essay first published in *Studio International* in 1969, in which Kosuth set out his stall for a purely conceptual art. In it, we find a transition from the negative questioning inherent in the aesthetic indifference of Duchamp's readymades to the positive 'investigations' of Kosuth's distinct brand of Conceptual art: a transition from the wide-eyed surprise of 'This is art?' to a new way of claiming 'This *is* art'.

Kosuth transformed the abstract negation of the aesthetic conception of art performed by the anti-art element of Duchamp's readymade into a *determinate* negation. He thereby transformed the *in*determinacy of Duchamp's generic conception of art into the determinacy of a new positivity: 'propositions as to art's nature'. Kosuth's 'pure' or 'theoretical' Conceptual art aspires to make a *new conceptual positivity* out of Duchamp's negations. As such it is dependent upon on a quite particular philosophy of language.[20]

The institutional conditions for this radical transcoding were established in the long, slow process of the reception of Duchamp's works into the art institution: in particular, the direct designation as 'art' of an object which had become so only as the result of a complex series of events surrounding its previous rejection (*Fountain*) – what we might call the *positivization of the readymade* – in conjunction with a whole array of new artistic developments which had taken place in reaction to American-type painting, involving a massive expansion of artistic means. This process effected a separation of two elements hitherto conjoined in the founding conflation of formalist modernism: *aestheticism* and *autonomy*. The former was rejected; the latter embraced. Duchamp's attack on the aesthetic definition of art was recouped within the institution by a generic conception of art which retained the notion of autonomy. Kosuth had already encountered a similar notion of autonomy within modernism, in Ad Reinhardt's understanding of monochrome painting as 'art as art'. In the wake of

LeWitt's essay, Duchamp's readymades were interpreted by Kosuth as an inversion of the logic of Reinhardt's understanding of monochrome painting: from the idea of 'art as art' to 'art as idea (as idea)'.[21] The crucial doubling registers the artistic enactment of the meta-artistic idea.

Kosuth received Duchamp's readymade into the context of Reinhardt's modernist idea of art as *autonomous* and hence *self-referential*. This is the second of the great conflations of formalist modernism, separated out by Kosuth from the first (the conflation of aestheticism and autonomy) and in this case maintained: the conflation of autonomy and self-referentiality. Ayer's logical positivist philosophy of language provided Kosuth with the means to think self-referentiality without the aesthetic. The positivism of Kosuth's understanding of Conceptual art is a consequence of the dual context of his joint reception of Duchamp's work and LeWitt's essay: Reinhard and logical positivism. For whereas Duchamp had maintained that 'there doesn't have to be a lot of the conceptual for me to like something. What I don't like is the completely nonconceptual, which is purely retinal; that irritates me'[22] – just as Lewitt had described the concept as no more than 'the most important aspect' of a Conceptual work – Kosuth and others came to aspire to the *completely*, autonomously and self-referentially, conceptual, to 'new *propositions* as to art's nature':

> Works of art are analytical propositions. That is, if viewed within
> their context – as art – they provide no information what-so-ever
> about any matter of fact. A work of art is a tautology in that it
> is a presentation of the artist's intention, that is, he is saying that
> a particular work of art *is* art which means, is a *definition* of art.
> Thus, that it is art is true a priori (which is what Judd means
> when he states that 'if someone calls it art, its art').

For Kosuth, Conceptual art is an art which *recognizes* that 'art's "art condition" is a conceptual state' – that is, that 'objects are conceptually irrelevant to the condition of art'. It is an art which is 'clearly conceptual in intent'.[23]

'Art After Philosophy' is one of the more technically confused philosophical statements about art. Yet it is exemplary – indeed, constitutive – in its illusion. In particular, it is an excellent illustration of the dependence of analytical or strong conceptual art upon specific (often highly problematic, but also inadvertently socially representative) philosophical standpoints: in Kosuth's case, the triumphant linguistic reductivism of a now long-discredited logical positivism. The *propositional* positivism of Kosuth's idea of art derives directly from A.J. Ayer, whose writings provided the medium for the translation of the formalist idea of autonomy as self-referentiality into the idiom of the analytical proposition. (After Wittgenstein, Kosuth assures us, '"Continental" philosophy need not seriously be considered'.[24]) At the same time, however, this propositional positivism is combined with a *psychological* positivism stemming from Kosuth's individualistic reading of Duchamp's nominalism – similar in many ways to LeWitt's stress on intentionality. For while the semantic positivity of Kosuth's idea of art appears to move decisively beyond LeWitt's psychologism, it is in fact held back, and tied to it, by his inflated conception of the stipulative power of the individual artist: art as 'a presentation of the artist's intention'. It is this combination which leads to the exaggeration of the cultural authority of the artist's critical discourse, characteristic of a certain sectarian Conceptualism; an exaggeration which is at once theoretical, strategic and opportunistic. It took the ultimate form of the attempt to efface the categorial difference between art and criticism in the polemical presentation of critical discourse as itself art, in the journal *Art-Language*, for example. There are thus three main components of Kosuth's conception: *linguistic reduction, psychologism,* and *the collapse of the distinction between art and criticism.*

Kosuth's self-understanding is marked by a fundamental equivocation about language. In search of an anti-aestheticist model for artistic autonomy, Kosuth hit upon the *analogy* of tautology: 'art is analogous to an analytical proposition'. However, lacking the resources to think the analogical, this soon collapsed into identity: 'Works of art *are* analytical propositions'.[25] Kosuth thus simultaneously introduced and foreclosed the issue of the semiological character of visual art, by abstracting from all questions of medium, form, visuality and materiality, while nonetheless continuing to pose them, implicitly, in his presumption of art's difference from other forms of signification. This is not a presumption that Kosuth has ever been able to redeem, theoretically. Yet this was in part his point: as the heir to empiricism, linguistic philosophy is anti-metaphysical, and philosophy of art was to be no exception. Rather than philosophy delineating art's realm, this was to be the job of art itself, in each instance, 'presenting new propositions as to art's nature'. By presenting different visual means of signifying the same propositional content, Kosuth's early works aim to demonstrate the independence of conceptual content from signifying form, in such as way as to make this show of independence into an (independent) propositional content of its own: Art as Idea as Idea. But what allows for these objects to be read in this way: as presentations of propositions about art's nature?

It is at this point that Kosuth's propositional positivism starts to break down. For on his account, an individual work of art – a material object – becomes 'a kind of proposition' within 'art's language' (rather than an object of aesthetic appreciation or a cultural object of some other kind) only when it is presented within what he calls 'the *context* of art'.[26] Yet the model of meaning to which the idea of an analytical proposition is tied is resolutely *anti*-contextual. The early Kosuth was thus forced to neutralize the contextualism in his own position in order to preserve the semantic purity of his Conceptualism. This is the function of his psychologism and the associated regression to the prioritization of artistic intention. For Kosuth, 'the context of art' (so rich in Duchamp) is reduced to no more than a space set aside for the realization of the artist's intention. Ultimately, it is the artist's intention that the work be understood as 'a comment on art' which makes it 'art'.

'This is a Portrait of Iris Clert if I say so' reads the famous telegram sent by Robert Rauschenberg to his dealer, Iris Clert, in 1961, as his contribution to an exhibition of portraits – simultaneously enacting and parodying this position. 'If someone calls it art, it's art', Donald Judd declared in 1965, rather more straightforwardly, as if bored by the obviousness of it all. And in 'Art After Philosophy', Kosuth quotes this phrase of Judd's twice. But who is the 'I' or the 'someone'? And how do they 'say' it or 'call' it? Kosuth's answer to this complex institutional question is a simple one, modelled on the *persona* of Duchamp: the 'I' or the 'someone' is an artist and an artist is someone (anyone) who 'questions the nature of art'. 'Art' is the product of the stipulating power of the individual artist, the individual questioner into the nature of art. The artist as author, in the sense of formative creator, is replaced by the (meta-) artist as nominator of artistic status. The death of the author becomes 'the birth of the artist as self-curator'.[27] This was one of the ways in which Duchamp's readymade was received in the USA in the late 1950s and early 1960s: in terms of an individualistic (indeed, voluntaristic) artistic nominalism. However, there was a crucial difference between Kosuth's situation and that of Duchamp (or even Rauschenberg, whose tongue, like Duchamp's, stayed in his cheek). For Kosuth, along with others of his generation, lacked a pre-established artistic persona, such as Duchamp had derived from his period of infamy as a painter. Their practice of self-curation was thus faced with the additional task of constructing artistic persona from scratch. Hence the importance of the critical, self-legitimating philosophical writings of the first generation of Conceptual artists to the status of their work as 'art': as guarantors and guardians of their right to nomination. The authority of philosophy was used to establish a right to nomination. Without this critical supplement, their nominations are unlikely to have been able to sustain their claims to legitimation.

It is the combination of conceptualism and intentionalism in Kosuth's conception of art which undermines the distinction between the work and the artist's critical discourse. For having established the legitimacy of the work as art through the analogy with propositional content, it was only a small step to making a similar claim for the discourse about it, since it too, paradigmatically, questions the nature of art. Art becomes the product of the artist's 'total signifying activity'.[28] Hence Seth Seigelaub's reversal of the distinction between 'primary' and 'secondary' information which allowed for the exhibition catalogue to take precedence over the exhibits:

> when art does not any longer depend upon its physical presence, when it has become an abstraction, it is not distorted and altered by its representation in books and catalogues. It becomes *primary* information, while the reproduction of conventional art in books or catalogues is necessarily *secondary* information. For example, a photograph of a painting is different from a painting, but a photograph of a photograph is just a photograph, or the setting of a line of type is just a line of type. When information is *primary*, the catalogue can become the exhibition *and* a catalogue auxiliary to it, whereas in the January 1969 show [held at 44 East 52nd St., New York, curated by Siegelaub] the catalogue was primary and the physical exhibition was auxiliary to it ... it's turning the whole thing around.[29]

But can the aesthetic dimension of the object be wholly disregarded in the drive towards 'propositional' content? Can the philosophical meaning of the work actually be wholly abstracted from its material means? Or to put it another way, can the constitutive ambiguity characteristic of the deployment of philosophy within the artistic field ever be finally resolved? One can be forgiven for doubting it. Especially in the light of the palpably aesthetic qualities of Kosuth's own work at the level of typography and design.

Kosuth's work attacked the aesthetic definition of the artwork in the name of linguistic meaning. According to Kosuth, art is not a question of morphology but a question of function. This distinction is reflected in Kosuth's distinction between a 'stylistic' Conceptualism which has failed to rid itself of residual morphological characteristics (in which Kosuth includes Robert Barry, Douglas Huebler, and Lawrence Weiner – the artists with which he was shown in Siegelaub's January 1969 show) and a 'purer' Conceptualism to which his own work, early Art & Language (Atkinson & Baldwin) and On Kawara are taken to belong. Yet his own work functioned largely by placing language *within* the visual field. How can visual representations of language be purified of the pre-aestheticized structures of handwriting and typographical design? Just as by the 1960s the products of Duchamp's early acts of aesthetic indifference had acquired a recognizable aesthetic dimension, so one is forced to conclude with Jeff Wall that:

> Kosuth ... presents the vestiges of the instrumentalized 'value-free' academic disciplines characteristic of the new American-type universities (empiricist sociology, information theory, positivist

language philosophy) in the fashionable forms of 1960s adver-
tising ... In this sense conceptualism is the *doppelgänger* of
Warhol-type 'Popism' in its helpless ironic mimicry, not of knowledge, but of the mechanisms of falsification of knowledge, whose
despotic and seductive forms of display are copied to make art
objects.[30]

In fact, directly contrary to his own self-understanding, we might say that
Kosuth enacts an *aestheticization of logical positivism*. His categorical
distinction between 'pure' and 'stylistic' Conceptualism cannot be sus-
tained. The question is not how to *eliminate* or *reduce* the aesthetic
dimension of the object (its morphological characteristics), but how, in
each instance, critically to regulate the play between 'aesthetic' and 'conceptual' terms. As the institutional history of the documentation of performance pieces and temporary works shows, it is an irreducible dimension
of the logic of the artistic field to present visual form, however attenuated
or seemingly irrelevant.

Kosuth used logical positivist philosophy of language as a guillotine to
eradicate the aesthetic dimension of the artwork. Art & Language, on the
other hand, increasingly became caught up in the intellectual seductions
of analytical philosophy as a self-sufficient cultural practice. If Kosuth
conceived art philosophically as propositional in nature, he nonetheless
continued to produce object-instantiated work as the means for the
communication of his propositions. Art & Language took a step back,
withdrawing to the immanent investigation of the logical structure of
language itself. In this respect, one might say, they were truer to the idea
of art as investigation than Kosuth himself.

Philosophy to the second degree: Art & Language

It is a perilous journey returning to the dense prose and contorted intellectualism of the now distant and strange world of the first six issues of the
journal *Art-Language* (May 1969–Summer 1972). Like documents
of a lost civilization, they demand and resist interpretation, appeal and
repulse, in equal measure. One finds oneself searching for a key, only to be
reminded that in this case the search *is* the key, and that they were no more
immediately intelligible in their own day than they are today.[31] Intellectual
difficulty, severity of expression, obsessive formalization, disjunctiveness
and incompleteness are all important aspects of the writing practice of the
Art & Language group, along with a certain self-deprecatingly aggressive
humour. Sub-cultural solidarity in the appreciation of difficulty for its own
sake has long been central to the appeal of professional philosophy to
outsiders. And this was a group who rapidly fell in love with the rituals
and techniques of rigour characteristic of logico-linguistic analysis in the

Anglo-American manner. The substantive point, however, is that unlike Kosuth, Art & Language appreciated the open character of philosophical inquiry as an ongoing task. Philosophy, for Kosuth, was essentially a set of *positions*; positions enabling of artistic practice, perhaps, but fixed positions nonetheless. With the keenness of the convert, Kosuth thought he knew what art was: propositions as to art's nature. Delving a little deeper, Art & Language wanted to know what propositions were, and that turned out to be somewhat more complicated than A.J. Ayer had led Kosuth to suspect.

Second, Art & Language sought to explore 'the possibilities of a theoretical analysis as a method for (possibly) making art'. (The parenthesis is typical of their prose.) That is, they were interested in the idea 'that an art form can evolve by taking as a point of initial inquiry the language-use of the art-society'.[32] In particular, they were mesmerized by the formal possibilities of various systems of meaning, in which the radical openness of purely logical possibility appears to have functioned as a utopian metaphor for the artistic and the social alike. This, then, was not 'art as philosophy', but philosophy as the possibility of a new kind of art, and hence, a new kind of society; perhaps even philosophy as itself a mode of conceptual art. Although by the fourth issue of the journal (November 1971), the expression 'so-called conceptual art' had begun to appear, alongside some fairly scathing philosophical remarks about Kosuth, the 'American Editor' of the second and third issues, once Conceptual art had established itself as a curatorial category.[33] Art & Language's own claim to the name Conceptual art would largely come later, as part of a self-serving – indeed, self-promoting – revisionist historiography of the movement.

The pursuit of philosophy, within its own terms, as the possible basis of a new kind of art practice simultaneously placed the group closer to the practitioners of the philosophical field – as co-workers in its enterprise – and distanced them from it, insofar as the 'publication' of their activities was conceived as a form of art practice, insulating them from the legitimating (and de-legitimating) mechanisms of the philosophical field itself. In other words, philosophy was culturally recoded according to the parameters of the artistic field, however deviant it may have been within it. In line with the cultural logic of autodidacticism, the group thus identified with institutional philosophy at the level of its investment in certain intellectual techniques, but disidentified at the level of its social form (professionalism). This led to a series of contradictory stances, regarding linguistic élitism, for example, creating a highly-strung ambivalence, relieved only in alternating bouts of critical aggression and defensive self-parody.[34] It is important to remember, though, that the formative context here was art-educational (with its connections to student politics), rather than the New York gallery world of Kosuth's 'investigations'. The parody was thus closer to the po-faced absurdism of Situationalism, than the cool irony of the artworld.[35]

These tensions were mediated through the development of the idea of an Art & Language conversational community (much like the community of investigators in C.S. Peirce's pragmatism), but the tensions between the philosophical, social, and artistic dimensions of the project made this a utopian quest. The pursuit of technical philosophical advances in logico-linguistic analysis at the level of the collective action of an artistic community could only be (and was retrospectively rationalized as) the metaphorical performance of a necessary failure. Meanwhile, the problem of the visual dimension of public display, which vitiates Kosuth's self-understanding, was to arise again as soon as the Art & Language project moved out of the spaces of its own community dispatches into the international artworld. Like Kosuth, Art & Language rapidly acquired a 'look', which conveyed a quite different social meaning to the one they intended.[36] In this regard, the *Documenta Index* of 1972 (a massive cross-referential index system, mapping relations of compatibility, incompatibility, and lack of relational value between its terms) is not the 'summary work of Conceptual Art' which Charles Harrison has claimed it to be (characteristically condensing the history of Conceptual art as a movement into the history of Art & Language),[37] but it is the summary work of Art & Language themselves in their development from 1968–1972. As such, it marks both the culmination and the demise of strong Conceptualism: the fantasy of the resolution of the constitutive ambiguity of philosophy's double-coding. Henceforth, the irreducible constitutive role of the visual in artistic meaning would be acknowledged, as the basis for a variety of new, frequently more directly political, artistic strategies, which would continue the battle against the modernist ideology of pure visuality in new, simultaneously 'visual' and 'conceptual' forms.

The vanishing mediator

What, then, are we to make of this odd philosophical interlude in the history of contemporary art which I have called exclusive or strong Conceptualism? It is tempting to treat it as either an aberration or a side-show: an alien intrusion into the artworld that has somehow managed to hijack large amounts of critical and art-historical space, vastly disproportionate to its significance, to the detriment of other kinds of Conceptual art. But this would be a mistake. The historical significance of an art practice bears no necessary relation to the statistical weight of its practitioners, or the temporal span of the practice. It depends more upon its catalytic and constitutive effects upon the meaning of subsequent practices than its ability to endure or even to succeed within its own terms. Such is the experimental nature of modern art. In this respect, analytical, exclusive or strong Conceptualism displays the character of what Max Weber called a vanishing mediator: in Jameson's gloss: 'a catalytic agent that permits an exchange of energies between two otherwise mutually exclusive terms . . . [and] serves . . . as a kind of overall bracket or framework within which change takes place and which can be dismantled and removed when its usefulness is over.'[38] More specifically, one might say, philosophy was the vanishing mediator in the transition from LeWitt's ontologically ambiguous, weak or inclusive Conceptualism to the generic conceptuality or post-Conceptual status of art since the mid-1970s. For in over-reacting to the absolutization of the aesthetic in the modernist ideology of pure visuality – by attempting the complete elimination of the aesthetic from the artistic field – theoretical or strong Conceptualism fulfilled the classically Hegelian function of exceeding a limit in such a way as to render it visible, thereby reinstituting it as a limit, on new grounds. It is the ironic historical function of theoretical or strong Conceptualism, through its identification with philosophy, to have reasserted the ineliminability of the aesthetic as a necessary element of the artwork, via a failed negation. At the same time, however, it also definitively demonstrated the radical insufficiency of this element to the meaning-producing capacity of the work. As such, it reaffirmed the constitutive ambiguity of philosophy's double-coding within the artistic field, as an enduring productive resource.

7

DIALOGUE WITH PSYCHOANALYSIS

There is no entry for 'philosophy' in the index of Jean Laplanche's *Essays on Otherness*.[1] Yet this is more indicative of its pervasiveness than its absence. Laplanche's psychoanalytical theorizing is in dialogue with philosophy to an unprecedented degree. It draws explicitly on the post-Kantian tradition of European philosophy in its painstaking reconstructions and critical developments of Freud's metapsychology in two main ways: first, in its situation of Freud's thinking on *seduction*, the *unconscious* and the *drives* in relation to the problematic of the philosophy of subjectivity in its development from Kant via Hegel to the early Heidegger (its analysis, it claims, is 'on the same terrain of being' as Heidegger's);[2] second, in its methodological reflections on the status and scope of Freud's concepts and interpretive practices.[3] Philosophy thus plays a dual role in Laplanche's thought as both the discursive terrain for the ontological generalization of Freud's insights and a second-order discourse in its own right. In each instance, it exhibits a distinctively French inflection. In the first case, there is the fusing of early Heideggerian and Hegelian perspectives, familiar since Kojève, in the characterization of the primacy of the other in terms of both a fundamental existential *questioning* and a constitutive *misrecognition*. Second, there is the conceptualization of theory-development in terms of the Bachelardian notion of *problematics* – relatively distinct conceptual fields, defined by structures of problems, which are characterized as much by the symptomatic absence of certain problems and concepts as they are by those that are visibly present.[4]

In each respect, something new is added to the received philosophies and their established combinations, not merely by the theoretical content of Freudian thought – the idea of the unconscious and its myriad consequences and implications – but through the elaboration of this content at the level of philosophical discourse itself. Thus, for example, with respect to the primacy of the other in the constitution of the human being as a simultaneously self-interpreting and sexual being (the central theme of his work), Laplanche employs a communication-based, translational re-thinking of the idea of misrecognition as 'enigmatic signification' which points towards a transformation of the ontological basis of pragmatics. While in his account of the spiral structure of the development of Freud's theory, as a double history of de-centring and re-centring, innovation and going astray, he highlights a tension inherent in theory-development in the human sciences, between the general-theoretical and practical-contextual functioning of concepts.

What follows reflects upon these connections of Laplanche's psycho-analytical theory to philosophical thought, with particular reference to their implications for the ontological status of Freudian metapsychology and the place and meanings of psychoanalytical concepts in cultural theory. First, however, let me lay out the bare bones of Laplanche's account of the ontological emergence of the human being as a de-centred subject out of the dynamics of the adult–child relation. Everything hinges on the *asymmetry* of the adult–child relationship and the *primacy of the other* in the constitution of the self. These two principles lead to an account of the formation of the human subject as a reaction to the 'implantation' of the unconscious desire of the adult in the child. Laplanche calls this account the 'general theory of seduction'. For Laplanche, psychoanalytical metapsychology is a general theory of seduction.[5]

The primacy of the other

There are a number of discrete elements in this account. The first is the fundamental *passivity* of the human infant as an entity dependent upon the adult for its biological self-preservation, and rooted as a social being in the communicational dimensions of its relations of self-preservation. The second is the idea of the adult as the site of the production of an *unconscious sexual desire* which necessarily cathects the infant in the course of the interactions which sustain it as a biological entity during the first year of its life. The third is the theorization of this cathexis as the *implantation* of a message – specifically, an 'enigmatic signification' – in the child which both demands translation and is untranslatable, since the child has no sense of desire beyond self-preservation, at this point. Laplanche refers to this situation as the 'primal communication situation'. The fourth element is a conceptualization of the reception of this impossible demand as a process of *primal repression*, in which the untranslatable, and consequently 'thing-like', aspects of the message are internalized to form the child's unconscious as an 'other within'. This is the 'metabolization' by the child of the primal communication situation. (Metabolization is always metabolization of the untranslatable.) As such it is at once defensive and constructive. It marks the inauguration of the child as an 'auto-theorizing', self-interpreting being and it leads to the constitution of the erogenous body (and auto-eroticism) out of the child's attempt to 'bind' the enigmatic signifiers. The constitution of the child's unconscious is thus coterminous with its production as a sexual being, with sexual drives distinct from, but 'leaning upon', its self-preservative instincts, and a fantasmatic mental structure (domain of representation) through which these drives are channelled. (The distinction between drive (*Treib*) and instinct (*Instinkt*) is crucial here, but remains invisible in the standard English translations of Freud in which *Treib* is rendered as 'instinct'.) The child thus becomes a 'subject' because of the manner in which it engages the desire of adults, and is *treated like* a subject, before it actually is one. Treating the child like a human subject *produces* the child as a (de-centred) subject, with an unconscious of its own.

The mysterious element in this process is the – presumably evolutionary – capacity inherent within the child so to metabolize the situation, prior to its subjectivation, or, in Laplanche's terminology, its capacity to be 'seduced'. To sum up Laplanche's position in a formula: *a human is a being that can be seduced*. That is, there is a basic susceptibility in the child to the 'peeling off' of sexuality from self-preservation by seduction, and hence to the emergence of a psychical domain of representation distinct from the immediately somatic. This capacity to metabolize enigmatic implantations appears, existentially, as a primal *questioning* or *openness* to the world of the human; a capacity for a type of recognition (recognition of the demand for translation inherent in the message) which precedes the production of the child as a subject, and hence, in Hegel's more narrowly cognitive terms, as a possible partner in recognition-relations. However, to say that the psychical-sexual dimension of human being is both derived from and distinct from the immediately somatic instinctual structure of self-preservation is not to imply that it is not, itself, in some way somatic. Rather, it is *mediately* so, via the drives, which mediate the realm of representation with the thing-like quality of de-signified signifiers. Hence the crucial role of the signifier as the 'thing-like' carrier of meaning. The ontological specificity of human being thus boils down to the production of the drives in the primal communication situation; the production of human subjectivity as fundamentally de-centred by the asymmetry of its relations with others. (In Laplanche's expression: the drives are a 'symptom' of the human being.) The alterity or otherness of the other is doubled here, since it is the otherness *within* the other (the adult's unconscious) which is the constitutive aspect of otherness at work in the process. Only the untranslatable is truly 'other'. That is, the dyadic adult–child relation only functions via a third term. This third is not added, serially, to the second, like Freud's 'father of personal prehistory', but constitutes the second *as* second (as other) by its difference from it, within it.

There are several advantages to this account of the emergence of human subjectivity, which I have sketched in only the crudest outline, and without reference to the important connections between identification, temporalization, and the death drive,[6] in comparison to the canonic philosophical models upon which it draws. First, the cognitivism of the Hegelian model of recognition/misrecognition is transformed by the affective, broadly ethical, communicational dimension of demand: the message's demand to be translated – a demand inherent in the communicational dimension of human relations as such.[7] The ethical structure of demand-and-response (abstracted, isolated, and absolutized by a thinker like Levinas into a mystical and ultimately ethically vacuous transcendence) is integrated with a cognitive model of representation, signification and translation, as ineliminably interwoven aspects of human life. Second, Laplanche provides a framework for locating this conjointly communicational and auto-theorizing form of being within a broader naturalism (self-preservation), from which it emerges, and to which it remains ultimately bound – one is tempted to say, 'in the last instance' – despite the *finite* transcendence of its psycho-sexual dynamics: fantasy. Finally, and methodologically most important for the argument of this book, this psychoanalytical model does not just represent an enrichment and mutual imbrication of the philosophical problematics of *questioning, recognition, feeling* and *communication*; it changes the status of the philosophical discourse on subjectivity, from the self-sufficiency of a self-grounding, reflective conceptual logic to something much closer to Marx's 1845 idea of a 'summing-up', or theoretical re-presentation from the standpoint of totality, of 'the most general results of the positive sciences' – shed of its more positivistic overtones. For these 'results' are not merely empirical generalizations, as Marx and Engels tended at that time to assume, but are themselves already deeply theoretically imbued with the conceptualizations of the analytical process.[8] That is to say, the acknowledgement of the opacity of the contents of the unconscious to the subject's normal consciousness, as 'the other thing in us', is associated with a critique of the philosophy of the subject as a self-sufficient discourse; indeed, with a critique of the self-sufficiency of any purely theoretical discourse. The question thus arises as to the specific form of universality (scope and limits) of such general psychoanalytical categories, situated as they are, in Freud's phrase, in 'a middle position between medicine and philosophy'[9] – philosophy, that is, in its modern disciplinary sense.

For Freud, the inaccessibility of dreams and the irreducibility of hypnosis to a rationalist model of consciousness required that we go beyond a self-reflexive analysis of mental life to seek a more adequate conception of the human subject in the new, empirically-based, but nonetheless still theoretical, form of 'psycho-analysis'. However, if prior philosophical analyses of psychic life appear, from this point of view, to indulge in the fantasy of *not having an unconscious*, such a fantasy also, paradoxically, seems to motivate psychoanalytical theory and practise themselves, in so far as they are oriented towards a maximal 'bringing to consciousness' on the part of analysands of unconscious representations. Treatment, on

Freud's model, aims to 'transform repetition into memory'.[10] It is in this sense that, in Michel Henry's words, Freud may be called the 'belated heir of Descartes', despite the fact that, as Lacan insisted, 'psychoanalysis *opposes* any philosophy issuing directly from the cogito'.[11] We are no longer in the situation described by Freud in *The Ego and the Id* (1923) when he wrote that:

> To most people who have been educated in philosophy the idea of anything psychical which is not also conscious is so inconceivable that it seems to them absurd and refutable simply by logic.[12]

No doubt, some who have been so educated still think thus. The philosophical consensus of contemporary theory is more likely to have moved beyond the reflective structure of consciousness as an ontological model for the psychic, to the broadly Nietzschean thesis of the fundamental *un*consciousness of the self or the purely fictional character of the cogito.[13] Nonetheless, Laplanche's psychoanalytical account of subjectivity remains a challenge to the self-sufficiency of philosophy, *whatever* the particular theoretical content of one's philosophy may be. Furthermore, given his emphasis on the pragmatic basis of Freud's concepts in therapeutic practice (specifically, the analytical situation), one might wonder how generalizable the model is beyond the horizon of that situation into broader fields of social and cultural analysis – Freud's own forays into these fields notwithstanding.[14]

The dialogue with philosophy in Laplanchean theory thus points in two different directions at once: *outward*s, towards a generalized psychoanalytical ontology of the human, which could provide the basis for work in other domains of the human sciences; *inwards*, towards a more limited conception of the contextual specificity of psychoanalytical concepts, as theoretical products of a highly specialized practice – psychoanalytical therapy – the legitimate application of which are bounded by the structural limits of that practice. In this latter case, legitimate generalization of such concepts would be restricted by the need for strictly analogous relations to other social domains. The competing sides of this dynamic of *ontological generalization* and *theoretical self-limitation* – can be explored with reference to Laplanche's account of the relationship between 'external' and 'internal' others.

Ontologization and social mediation

There has been much loose talk about 'the other' in recent cultural analysis – be it Lacanian, Levinasian or, in the case of postcolonial studies, part of a phenomenological anthropology. Indeed, increasingly, one finds allusions to all three forms of otherness at once. And while it probably has not cost any lives (victory in the academic theatre of the culture wars is judged by other means), it has caused considerable confusion. One particular cause of confusion has been a slippage between philosophically or psychoanalytically defined, internal symbolic conceptions of otherness, on the one hand, and a variety of phenomenological forms of recognition of actually historically existing differences between social groups, on the other. Indeed, one might go so far as to suggest that the use of Lacanianism in social and cultural theory is *premised* on a slippage between the socio-symbolic and the Lacanian Symbolic; while the use of Levinas in this area often depends upon a similar conflation of the absolute alterity at stake in his work with socio-historically specific forms of 'otherness' or difference. (This follows from the misapprehension that Levinas was interested in ethics – an ethics 'of' otherness – rather than with 'the ethical' as such, in a sense that is actually ethically indeterminate.)

It is the advantage of Laplanchean theory that it sets out from a clear distinction between 'internal' and 'external' others, and offers an account of their mutual relations. Indeed, if there is a polemical thought associated with the Laplanchean version of the primacy of the other in the constitution of the human subject it can be summed up programmatically as: 'Against Freudian Ipso-centrism'! This is its difference from Object Relations theory. There are many different 'others', but they are distributed across these two fundamentally distinct domains. On Laplanche's account: 'The other person [that is, the external other] is primal in relation to the construction of human subjectivity';[15] while the internal or psychical other – the other 'thing' in our unconscious – is derived. Analysis 'goes back along the thread of th[is] 'other': [from, i] the other thing of our unconscious, [to, ii] the other person who has implanted his [or her] messages, with, as horizon, [iii] the other thing in the other person, that is, the unconscious of the other, which makes those messages enigmatic';[16] and one might add, [iv] the third persons who have implanted their messages in the unconscious of the other person, etc. I see no need to curtail this regress (other than empirically) or, indeed, to retain the dyadic structure (other than transcendentally), even though this dyad is, in any case, already a triad, because of the doubling of otherness within the external other by their own 'internal' otherness.

'How much work?', and 'what kind of work?' can this distinction between 'internal' and 'external' others do in the critical extension of pyschoanalytical categories beyond both the hegemonic social scripts which they classically embody (the castration complex, for example) and the biographical situation of individuals, into more nuanced but nonetheless generalized forms of cultural and historical analysis. This depends, in part, upon the level of abstraction at which one locates the process of ontological generalization. What look at first sight like two rather different alternatives present themselves.

The first alternative would emphasize the empirical openness of Laplanche's model of the 'primal communication situation' to the implantation of a variety of unconscious desires by a variety of adults, to take psychoanalytical account of a plurality of cultural scripts from the very beginning of the infant's life. In particular, one might emphasize the secondary or derived character of sexual difference, opening up the joyous space of a non-Lacanian mode of psychoanalytical cultural study, amenable to certain of the theoretical insights of queer theory and the recognition of the importance of sibling relations. Generalization would take place here via the multiplication of socio-historical mediations, on the basis of a recognition of the *under*determination of the 'ontic', or actually existing, forms of subjectivity by the formal ontological model of child–adult asymmetry. The cultural overdetermination of the contradictory experience of *passivity*, for example, (contradictory, because no experience can be wholly passive) would move to the fore.[17] The advantage of the Laplanchean model, from this point of view, is its formalism, opening up a space for the mediation of psychoanalytical and socio-historical categories.

The difficulty here concerns the symbolic power and social weight of the hegemonic forms of subjectivity produced by the generational 'thread of others', and reproduced by the force of established social norms, irrespective of innovations in social practices within a single generation.[18] In the formation of subjectivity, the notion of the external other marks the empirical moment of historical openness, while the internal other marks that of consolidation, or the psychic fixing of certain received structures of relations. However, it is the external other's internal other (the adult's unconscious) which is the source of enigmatic signifiers. Primal communication is thus always across *three*, not two, generations. From this point of view, the psychic dimension of sexual politics appears in its harshest but most realistic historical form as a *multiply transgenerational* project. What remains obscure is the range of practicable possibilities for new forms of relations between adults associated with the myriad of positional possibilities inherent in the structure of identifications posited in Freud's notion of primal fantasy.[19] For some, it is tempting, under these circumstances, to opt for the second alternative.

The second alternative would stress that while the ontological model of the implantation of enigmatic signifiers via child–adult asymmetry is indeed articulated at a certain level of formality, there is nonetheless sufficient transhistorical content built into the psychoanalytical elaboration of the 'standard form' of the primal communication situation (with the breast as the paradigmatic enigmatic signifier) to provide a quasi-ontological groundwork for cultural theory, with considerable powers of ontic determination. As Laplanche himself has put it: 'one has the right to be somewhat pessimistic'.[20] Hence the peculiar phenomenon of Lacanian feminism, which involves the adoption of a theoretical model which pathologizes and denies the realizable possibility of the politics it purports to inform. However, given the rejection of the self-sufficiency of philosophical discourse as self-grounding universality, methodologically, the difference between the two alternatives is largely one of degree. One is free to reject the ontologization of sexual difference, for example, on conventional empirical-explanatory grounds. Either way, whichever approach one takes, Laplanchean theory distinguishes itself from the wilder metaphorical applications of psychoanalyical theory dominant in contemporary cultural analysis, epitomized by Jameson's casual extension of the notion of schizophrenia to describe an allegedly 'postmodern' form of subjectivity, *tout court*, and Zizek's unrelenting readings of ideological movements and political events in the direct, unmediated, psychically reductive terms of a substantivist psychoanalytical ontology – currently, predominantly, through the 'plague of fantasies'.[21] However, both of the forms of generalization that I have suggested are threatened by the methodological strictures stemming from the primacy of the analytical situation in the elaboration of psychoanalytical categories.

Theoretical self-limitation or universal transference?

Where do psychoanalytical concepts come from? The question is harder than it looks. Laplanche suggests a 'spiral' model of the development of Freud's theory in which two apparently contradictory problematics – one 'Copernican' or de-centring, based on the primacy of the external other, the second 'Ptolemaic' or re-centring, enclosed within the intrapsychic domain of representation – compete for explanatory power. However, his own account of their contest actually renders them commensurable, since the 'Ptolemaic' recuperation of the 'Copernican', and the latter's subsequent reassertion, are ultimately read as a dynamic structure homologous to the contradictory structure of human subjectivity itself. There is a higher-level coherence which suggests a 'fusing' of opposed approaches in a new meta-problematic, a breakdown or at least a supersession of the Ptolemaic–Copernican metaphor itself. (The relationship of Newtonian physics to relativity theory, with the former incorporated as an approximation with the latter, would be a better analogy.) This is apparent in the fact that while Laplanche privileges the de-centring, Copernican approach of the primacy of the external other, he nonetheless acknowledges the 'Ptolemaic' perspective of re-centring to be constitutive of the specific object of psychoanalytical theory: that is, 'the human subject *in so far as* that subject is auto-hypothetical, auto-conjectural, auto-representative, and auto-theorizing'.[22] As such, the movement of de-centring (via the external other) only ever *appears* within the more centred approach, as an internal displacement, recovered, negatively, so to speak, from within the subject's system of representations. This is a consequence of the basis of the theory in the therapeutic practice of psychoanalysis as a mediated form of *self-treatment*: treatment of the self by the self via the relationship to the analyst.[23]

In the analytical situation, the analyst doesn't try to gather information about the patient's external others from external sources (although Freud himself was not adverse to doing this, on occasion, in order to 'support' self-interpretation with 'anticipatory ideas'), since the patient can only *work* with their own representations – representations which carry the charge of a buried history of investments. This would appear to mortgage the metapsychological concepts derived from the therapeutic practice to the dynamics of the analytical situation, which make the analysand's recovery of repressed material possible. Thus, while philosophical concepts and structures of argument might contribute to theory-formation, in the working up of material from the analytical situation into more general metapsychologcial concepts, it cannot be claimed that the results of this process occupy a genuinely ontological terrain ('the same terrain of being' as Heidegger's) unless – and this is the crucial point – there is something not just 'humanly universal', but *fundamentally* or paradigmatically 'humanly universal', about the analytical situation itself. This is precisely what Laplanche claims in his discussion of transference.

Transference is the strange process by which, according to Freud, what 'seemed in every case to constitute the greatest threat to the treatment becomes its best tool, by whose help the most secret compartments of mental life can be opened': the transference onto the analyst by the analysand of the 'intense feelings' of libidinal object-cathexes. For the transference *renders visible* the unconscious processes of condensation and displacement that produce symptoms as substitute satisfactions of the libido; renders them visible to both the analyst and (potentially) the analysand alike. Indeed, Freud remarks, his 'conviction of the significance of symptoms as substitute satisfactions of the libido only received its final confirmation after the enlistment of the transference'. The transference thus produces 'a new edition of the old disorder', a 'newly created and transformed neurosis' in relation to which the patient's symptoms abandon their original meaning and take on a new sense. It is by mastering this 'new, artificial neurosis' that the original illness is treated.[24] Psychoanalytical therapy treats the condition by treating the resistances to its treatment which it, the therapy, itself provokes. Transference is a special, enabling form of resistance. All transference is transference-resistance (*Übertragungswiderstand*).

Freud acknowledged the universality of the phenomenon:

> A capacity for directing libidinal object-cathexies on to people must of course be attributed to every normal person. The tendency to transference of the neurotics I have spoken of is only an extraordinary increase of this universal characteristic.

And he described it as a general 'suggestibility', noting that 'in our technique we have abandoned hypnosis only to rediscover suggestion in the
shape of transference'. However, while Freud considered transference to
'depend on' sexuality, he offered no further elaboration of either the
reasons for its generality or the specificity of the analytical situation as
its privileged site, the analyst as its privileged point.[25] (For Freud, it is in
the specificity of the neurotic that the specificity of analytical transference
resides – not the analyst or the relationship of analyst to analysand.)
Laplanche fills these lacunae by relocating transference within the terms
of the general theory of seduction. Transference is *analytical seduction*.[26]

> Transference . . . is characteristic of the analytical situation and
> of some other specific intersubjective constellations which all have
> in common the fact that they reproduce and renew the situation
> of primal seduction . . . the primary situation of the drive is a
> relation . . . of transference . . . since the whole movement of
> symbolization consists in adding new signifiers with the purpose
> of displacing, transposing and thus binding the most traumatic
> signifiers. Transference . . . can only be the continuation or resump-
> tion of this movement of symbolization . . . the reopening of the
> primal transference.[27]

The primal communication situation is a primal transference. Transference
is 'a relationship with the enigmatic object'. It is for this reason that it
can have no end. The only conceivable end for an analysis is a 'transference of transference': a new set of symbolizations which bind the most
traumatic/enigmatic signifiers in a new, less compulsive way.[28]

What this relocation of the ontological basis of transference in the
primal situation (relation to the enigma of the other) implies, according
to Laplanche, is that:

> perhaps the principal site of transference, 'ordinary' transference,
> before, beyond or after analysis, would be the multiple relation
> to the cultural, to creation or, more precisely, to the cultural
> message. A relation which is multiple, and should be conceived
> with discrimination, but always starting from the relation to the
> enigma.[29]

Those 'other specific intersubjective constellations' which share the structure of transference with the analytical situation are those of the
production, reception and analysis of 'cultural messages'; that is, messages
which are addressed to an *indeterminate* cultural other. All cultural products address 'an other who is out of reach' and are received by those to
whom they were not specifically addressed. Culture is the site of a generic

otherness (an other within the otherness of the cultural product) which both demands and resists translation. That is, it is 'the site of an enigmatic interpellation' which constantly re-opens the originary relation of the primacy of the other. In this respect, artistic creation is less sublimation than transference.[30] This explains the 'transference of the transference' which is the only conceivable end to an analysis. The analytical transference is transferred to other cultural sites.

The difference between the two kinds of site (analytical and cultural) concerns the balance between what Laplanche distinguishes as two basic types or aspects of transference: 'hollowed out' transference and 'full' or 'filled in' transference. In the analytical situation, the analyst creates what Laplanche thinks of as a hollowed-out communicational space, by virtue of his or her refusal to know. The analyst is the one who is *supposed to know* (like the adult for the child), but who *refuses to know*. As such he or she recreates the primal communication situation in which the analysand/child reacts to the anxiety provoked by the enigma of the address of the other. Hollow transference occupies this space in such a way as to retain its openness or hollowed out character, by regaining and retaining the enigmatic character of the primal situation; filled in transference involves 'a positive reproduction of forms of behaviour, relationships and childhood imagos'.[31] (Freud's conception of transference is one which is always filled in.) Hollow transference would thus seem to correspond to the moment of de-translation/dissolution of the manifest translations/ symbolizations of the analysand's speech; filled in transference to the moment of binding that alleviates the anxiety by producing new translations/symbolizations. In cultural messages in general, the cultural product occupies the position equivalent to the analyst in the analytical situation and the adult in the primal situation. How 'hollowed out' any particular cultural site is, and how hollow or filled in the transference connected to any particular cultural product, will depend upon the former's institutional structure and the latter's specific form. However, one is tempted to see in the institutional construction of artistic autonomy the cultural site most directly analogous to the hollowed out space of the analytical situation – although Laplanche himself has not extended his analysis in this direction, as far as I am aware.[32]

Psychoanalysis and cultural experience

We are now in a position to return to the issues from which we set out: the ontological status of the categories of metapsychology and the place and meanings of psychoanalytical concepts in cultural theory. The ontological generalization of the insights of the analytical situation depends upon how fundamentally or paradigmatically 'human' that situation can be shown to be. Laplanche has attempted to establish the requisite fundamental human universality by the argument that the analytical situation replicates the structure of the primal communication situation out of which human subjectivity emerges. To the extent to which this argument is accepted, the pragmatic context of psychoanalytical knowledge turns out to be, not so much a limitation on its universality, as the *ground* of its specific universality: the domain of the unconscious determination of human action by psychic structures and processes formed in early childhood. However, there is a danger of circularity here, since the analytical situation is itself the means of access to the primal situation, which is thus a *construction* of psychoanalysis, in the sense that, for Freud, construction is to be distinguished from, and exceeds, interpretation.[33] However, the construction of the primal situation is neither a spontaneous act of theoretical creativity nor a simple process of the generalization of empirical data (case histories), but rather a procedure of general-theoretical modelling that draws heavily upon the conceptual resources of the philosophical tradition. The criteria of adequacy of such a model are empirical only in the proper, expanded sense that includes its compatibility with, and capacity to integrate, existing large-scale bodies of historical, cultural, social scientific and medical knowledge (relative to competing models); not to mention the classical theoretical virtues of internal consistency and simplicity. Nonetheless, for all its hypothetical universality (a hypothetical character it shares with all 'scientific', as opposed to 'strictly philosophical', ontologies), the pragmatic basis of the model renders its universality perspectival relative to other forms or levels of explanation of human behaviour (economic, political, etc.) with which its accounts must consequently be mediated in any more general explanatory situation. It is this mediation that has consistently been so hard to achieve, leading to either reductive or metaphorical applications of psychoanalytical categories in both the social sciences and the humanities.

However, the communicational form of the universality implicit in the analytical situation links psychoanalytical concepts *directly* to the analysis of other communication situations but in a rather different manner from the way in which such concepts are normally used in cultural analysis. This difference may be summed up in Laplanche's remark: 'The theory of seduction is not a reading "language", but an attempt to understand analytical practice.' Indeed, he insists, 'what is known as a "psychoanalytical reading", whose banality we are sick and tired of, is a direct means of repression'.[34] (Certain strands of Anglo-American film and literary theory of the 1980s, and the repetitive structure of Zizek's work, in particular, spring readily to mind.) 'Psychoanalytical readings' are a means of repression to the extent that they shield the reader from the productive enigma of the text/object/practice by imposing a standardized narrative interpretation: the Oedipal reading, the 'depressive position' reading, the Real reading. ... Such readings offer the comfort, not of strangers, but of all-too-familiar *codings* of strangeness which serve to reinforce the inter-preting subject's existing formation. As such, they offer a theoretical version of the pleasure in repetition which is an essential part of all cultural experience. 'Again! Again!', as the Teletubbies say. This is not *in itself* a 'bad thing', of course. I do not mean to invoke a psychoanalytical version of the moralism that so often accompanies the valorization of the singu-larity of the experience of autonomous art – the condemnation of repetition as regression. (Singularity is as readily fetishized as anything else.) We are all Teletubbies: that is the point, of psychoanalysis and *Teletubbies* alike. However, it is a problem, this repetition of the familiar, in so far as we aspire to distinguish critical-theoretical analyses of culture from first-order cultural experience. What Laplanche's approach to the generalization of psychoanalytical categories beyond the analytical situation suggests is that this difference cannot be established by the presence or absence of theo-retical content within interpretation (all experience is theoretically imbued, as Freud's essay 'The Sexual Theories of Children' makes plain enough); it can only be established by the pragmatic character or *communicational form* of the relation to the object. This can be elaborated with reference to the way in which Laplanche's distinction between two different levels of theory maps onto a distinction between recipients and critical analysts of cultural messages.

Laplanche distinguishes between 'the theories discovered in the human being by psychoanalysis' (Level 1) – such as the sexual theories of chil-dren – and 'specifically psychoanalytical theory' (Level 2), which purports to provide an epistemologically superior account of its object, in part, by giving an account of the production of theories at Level 1. This is straight-forward enough and would be uncontentious were it not for the fact that the majority of psychoanalysts and, one might add, psychoanalytical cultural theorists, have taken various Level 1 theories and 'made them their *own* theories'. Take the castration complex, for example, which psychoanalysis claims to have discovered in children as their way of explaining to themselves the enigma of gender. This is a fantasmatic cultural code. Yet how easily, with Lacanianism, it becomes 'the psycho-analytical theory of sexual difference', condemning its adherents to the illusions of childhood sexuality in perpetuity. The difference is crucial, not only because of the explanatory claims at stake, but also because of the pragmatic context which determines their respective functions. On the Laplanchean model, it is the function of childhood theories to diminish the anxiety produced by enigmatic signifiers; in much the same way that it is the function of ideologies to provide imaginary resolutions to contra-dictions which remain practically irresolvable within a given set of social relations. It is the function of psychoanalytical theory, on the other hand, to provide an account of otherwise inexplicable behaviour and forms of experience, in order to help guide that behaviour/experience into less destructive forms. The main way it does this is by giving an account of the enduring significance of the character and function of the theories at Level 1; in practice, by leading the analysand back to them, through the unbinding effects of the method of free association.[35]

This distinction between two levels of theory can be transposed to the analysis of cultural messages by distinguishing between the interpreting recipient of cultural messages (Level 1) and the critical analyst (Level 2) who gives an account of the messages, in part, by reflecting upon the basis of the standard interpretations in play at Level 1. The complication is that just as the analyst is him- or herself a human being with an unconscious that he/she cannot control (a fact from which psychoanalysis is in constant retreat: the desire of the analyst), so the cultural analyst is him- or herself an interpreter of cultural messages at Level 1. Indeed, it is via their role as recipients of cultural messages at Level 1 that cultural analysts acquire their materials for analysis, just as it was via his relation to his own childhood (self-analysis) that Freud founded psychoanalysis. The role of the (psychoanalytical) cultural analyst is thus doubled in a way which is often conflated in practice. The cultural analyst is at once 1) a reader/interpreter and member of the community of recipients (most criticism is a refined version of this role); and 2) an analyst of the messages at another level, via a different theoretical problematic. The difficulty with the analogy – or the point at which it is most strained – concerns the pragmatic dimension. For what is the cultural equivalent of the interactional dynamic of analytical transference by which the psychoanalyst helps guide the analysand towards self-knowledge and thereby away from destructively repetitive forms of experience/behaviour?

When Laplanche writes of the 'transference of the transference' as the end of analysis, he evokes a transference between the (ex)analysand and the cultural message, which presupposes an end to analytical intervention. However, the analogy between psychoanalysis and cultural *analysis*, with the two levels of theory, reopens the question of pragmatic function: the function of a psychoanalytical cultural analysis relative to the function of cultural experience or the interpretive reception of cultural messages in general. This is too vast and complex a topic to treat in any detail here. Let me end, however, by gesturing towards an approach suggested by the place of 'analysis' (in a strict but general conceptual sense) within the process of transference.

Etymologically, 'analysis' is constituted by the combination of two motifs in the Greek *analuein*:

> There is, *on the one hand*, what could be called the *archeo-logical* or *anagogical* motif, which is marked in the movement of *ana* (recurrent return towards the principal, the most originary, the simplest, the elementary, or the detail that cannot be broken

down); and, *on the other hand*, a motif that could be nicknamed *lytic*, *lytological*, or *philolytic*, marked in the *lysis* (breaking down, untying, unknotting, deliverance, dissolution or absolution, and, by the same token, final completion).[36]

This is reflected within the analytical situation in the double movement of the analyst leading the analysand *back* to repressed memories, through the *unbinding or dissolutive* effects of the method of free association. In a manner which appears to be modelled on Freud's positing of two fundamentally opposed drives (eros and the death drive), Derrida understands this dual movement as a doubling of the archaeological motif by 'an eschatological movement, as if analysis were the bearer of extreme death and the last word, as the archaeological motif, in view of the originary, is turned towards birth'.[37] This is neatly symmetrical, but in so far as it associates dissolution (*Lösung*) with the 'last word', it misrepresents the dynamics of the analytical process as a whole. For analysis, in this general but strict conceptual sense, is only part of the movement of transference. Its two-fold eschatological and archaeological movement is supplemented by a process of rebinding; just as, classically, in philosophy, the analytical method is complemented by synthesis – a process of unification which Kant would come to identify with the constitution of experience itself. (In fact, the analytical process has a structure not unlike the phenomenological movement of *The Critique of Pure Reason* itself.)

Correspondingly, one might say that the function of a psychoanalytical cultural analysis, as the structural equivalent of the application of Level 2 psychoanalytical theory, is to disrupt the standard cultural interpretations of Level 1 theory, by breaking them down into their constituent elements, drawing attention to their translations and to the associated repressions of the enigmatic aspects of the messages, thereby opening the space for the cultural equivalent of rebinding: new interpretations/forms of cultural experience more adequate to the Level 2 account of the function of the messages. The point, though, is that if it is to remain true to the pragmatic basis or communicational form of its concepts, such a mode of cultural analysis cannot secure the epistemological status of new interpretations itself, *qua* Level 2 theory. Rather, it must have its interpretations produced by the recipients via their transferential relationship to the cultural messages of the analysis. In fact, in so far as the cultural analyst him- or herself propounds a new interpretation or construction – out of the theoretical account of the message via an analysis of standard interpretations – he or she returns to the community of recipients/interpreters (Level 1), as a kind of meta-interpreter.

There is thus a fundamental ambiguity about the epistemological status of the interpretive dimension of psychoanalytical cultural analysis which follows directly from the structure of the analogy upon which it is based. For not only is there no apparent equivalent to the analyst/ analysand relationship, but nor does there appear to be any direct equivalent to the analytical process as a form of self-treatment through *self-knowledge*; except in so far as any cultural message carries with it, in the indeterminacy of its address, a certain universal potential for self-recognition in otherness. But even here, the character of the 'self' in question remains obscure. There is, furthermore, an ideological dimension to the 'transference of the transference' – questions about the social function of cultural transference, relative to different kinds of messages in different kinds of society – which indicate that a psychoanalytical cultural theory can only operate in conjunction with other (economic and political) forms of analysis.

This is only a sketch of some of the problems that arise when one begins to take the communicational dimension of the analogical basis of psychoanalytical cultural analysis seriously. It is the virtue of Laplanche's work to draw attention to this dimension at a time when the use of psychoanalytical concepts in cultural analysis is overwhelmingly merely interpretive (Level 1). For the object of a psychoanalytical cultural analysis cannot be cultural messages (texts/objects/practices) alone, but must rather be the relationship of such messages to the interpretations and interpretive theories through which they are most commonly received: that is, cultural *experience* in the full sense of the term.

NOTES

PREFACE

1 *Times Higher Education Supplement*, 21 June 1996 and 31 January 1997.
2 I owe this formulation of my practice as a type of reflective judgement to Howard Caygill.

1 PHILOSOPHY IN CULTURAL THEORY

1 Cf. Richard Rorty, 'Introduction', *Consequences of Pragmatism (Essays: 1972–1980)*, Harvester Press, Brighton, 1982, p. xiv.
2 Alasdair MacIntyre, 'Philosophy: Past Conflict and Future Direction', *Proceedings of the American Philosophical Association*, Supplement to Vol. 61, no. 1, September 1987, p. 81.
3 Immanuel Kant, *The Conflict of the Faculties* (1798), trans. Mary J. Gregor, Nebraska University Press, Lincoln and London, 1979. Regarding the traditional nomenclature, Kant points out that 'a faculty is considered higher only if its teachings ... interest the government itself', p. 25.
4 Ibid., p. 45.
5 Theodor W. Adorno, *Negative Dialectics* (1966), trans. E.B. Ashton, Routledge, London, 1973, p. 3.
6 'Why Still Philosophy?', in Theodor W. Adorno, *Critical Models: Interventions and Catchwords*, trans. Henry W. Pickford, Columbia University Press, New York, 1998, pp. 5–17.
7 The decisive shift in argumentative form followed in the wake of Hegel's temporalization of totality as history, and the subsequent critique of absolute idealism's ultimate eternalization or de-temporalization of the newly temporalized form. See Peter Osborne, 'One Time, One History?', *The Politics of Time: Modernity and Avant-Garde*, Verso, London and New York, 1995, ch. 2.
8 '... there neither is, nor can be, a science of the beautiful', Immanuel Kant, *Critique of Judgement*, trans. Werner S. Pluhar, Hackett, Indianapolis/Cambridge, 1987, p. 230.
9 Tom Steele, *The Emergence of Cultural Studies, 1945–1965: Adult Education, Cultural Politics and the English Question*, Lawrence & Wishart, London, 1997, p. 7.
10 'Culture and Power: An Interview with Stuart Hall', *Radical Philosophy* 86 (November–December 1997), p. 27: 'What was there as philosophy wasn't of any help to us in a pragmatic sense.'

11 For critiques of the ethnic nationalism implicit in Williams's conception of a common culture, see Paul Gilroy, *There Ain't No Black in the Union Jack: The Cultural Politics of Race and Nation*, Hutchinson, London, 1987, pp. 49–50 and 'Cultural Studies and Ethnic Absolutism', in Lawrence Grossberg, Cary Nelson and Paula A. Treichler (eds.), *Cultural Studies*, Routledge, London and New York, 1992, pp. 187–98; and Stuart Hall, 'Culture, Community, Nation', *Cultural Studies* 7 (1994), pp. 349–363. This problem is inherent in the very idea of individual 'cultures' inherited from nine-teenth-century anthropology, and reproduced, despite itself, in much recent postcolonial theory and 'new ethnography'. Nonetheless, one should not under-estimate the democratic potential of the term 'ordinary' to motivate critical transformations of its more restricted, hegemonic uses. Culture is ordinary, one might say, but what is ordinary is often very far from being common. As Gilroy notes ('Ethnic Absolutism', p. 190), the entry of black people into national life was a powerful factor in the formation of cultural studies in Britain. If politics is a practice of *making* common, it has difference as its condition.

12 Cf. Kate Soper, 'Despairing of Happiness: The Redeeming Dialectic of Critical Theory', *New Formations*, no. 38 (Summer 1999), *Hating Tradition Properly: The Legacy of the Frankfurt School in Cultural Studies*, p. 142. More generally, see Helmut Dubiel, *Theory and Politics: Studies in the Development of Critical Theory*, trans. Benjamin Gregg, MIT Press, Cambridge, MA, 1984, and Rolf Wiggershaus, *The Frankfurt School*, trans. Martin Robinson, Polity Press, Cambridge, 1994. Dubiel's study covers the period from 1930 to 1945, by which time the dynamic relations between interdisciplinary research, theory construc-tion, dialectical presentation, and political projection had been stilled by the overdetermining sway of the critique of instrumental reason. In its classical form, 'critical theory' was formulated during the brief second phase of this period, 1937–1940, following on from and summing up the more open first phase of 'interdisciplinary materialism', 1930–1937. Cf. Marx's idea of the replacement of 'self-sufficient' philosophy with 'a summing-up of the most general results' of the positive sciences, in *The German Ideology* (1845–6), Karl Marx and Frederick Engels, *Collected Works*, Vol. 5, Lawrence and Wishart, London, 1976, p. 37.

13 Cf. Herbert Schnädelbach, 'The Cultural Legacy of Critical Theory', in *New Formations* no. 38, pp. 64–6. Habermas's attempt to revive Horkheimer's project of a critical theory via the Nietzschean neo-Kantianism of knowledge-constitutive interests (constituting a critical science through an emancipatory interest) cuts off the dialectical cross-disciplinarity of the original at its source. See Jürgen Habermas, *Knowledge and Human Interests* (1968), trans. Jeremy J. Shapiro, Heinemann, London, 1972. His subsequent idea of philosophy as rational reconstruction – 'stand-in and interpreter' – replaces the (negative) Hegelian aspirations of Horkheimer's original with an aspiration to the prac-tical articulation of fundamentally differentated value-spheres. The only legitimate role for the category of totality is taken to lie in the phenomeno-logical structure of the 'lifeworld', where it is 'implicit', 'prereflexive' and 'only known subconsciously', Jürgen Habermas, *Postmetaphysical Thinking*, trans. William Mark Hohengarten, Polity Press, Cambridge, 1992, pp. 142–3. The consequent disjunction between lifeworld and system (the institutional real-ization and functional articulation of the value-spheres) is subject to a ban on theoretical mediation, out of fear of the objectivistic fallacy. The elimination of the dialectical cross-disciplinarity of the original version is thus accompa-nied by a corresponding separation of theory from politics.

14 With the important exception of the interest in Althusser's concept of overde-
termination. 'Contradiction and Overdetermination' (1962), in Louis Althusser,
For Marx, trans. Ben Brewster, New Left Books, London, 1977, pp. 87–128.
For the early Williams, the totalizing structure of the project was not so much
to be theoretically constructed as *recognized* as co-extensive with culture itself:
'the relations between elements in a whole way of life', Raymond Williams,
Culture and Society 1780–1950, Penguin, Harmondsworth, 1961, pp. 11–12.
As Mulhern has pointed out, for Williams, late as well as early, culture 'is
not the whole, nor is it only coextensive with the whole; it is, rather, the principle of *whole-ness* in social life. Culture is more than a specific object of
inquiry: it is the qualifying condition of all fruitful social analysis and judgement', Francis Mulhern, *Culture/Metaculture*, Routledge, London and New
York, 2000, pp. 89–90. It is this metacritical principle of culture as wholeness that associates Williams with the tradition of *Kulturkritik*, which is the
topic of the first part of Mulhern's book. Unfortunately, Mulhern's incisive
study, which offers a comparative analysis of *Kulturkritik* and cultural studies,
and a diagnosis of their underlying 'metacultural' identity, omits the Frankfurt
School.

15 In Jameson's case, the connection to struturalism is particularly clear. See
Fredric Jameson, *The Prison-House of Language: A Critical Account of
Structuralism and Russian Formalism*, Princeton University Press, Princeton,
1972.

16 See Fredric Jameson, 'On "Cultural Studies"', *Social Text* 34 (1993), pp. 17–52.
Jameson appropriates Lyotard's formulation, 'the desire called Marx', to inter-
pret cultural studies as a structure of desire.

17 Peirce, 'How to Make our Ideas Clear', in *Philosophical Writings of Peirce*,
edited by Justus Buchler, Dover, New York, 1955, p. 31. In fact, Peirce
nowhere uses the term 'pragmatism' or even the adjectival 'pragmatic' in this
paper, although he retrospectively claimed invention of the name, with reference to the rule, over 25 years later, in his paper 'What Pragmatism Is' (1905),
following William James's attribution of it to him in the lecture 'Philosophical
Conceptions and Practical Results', seven years previously. Whatever its precise
provenance, the word was part of the lingua franca of discussions of the 'half-
ironically, half-defiantly' named Metaphysical Club, which Peirce founded
along with William James in Cambridge Massachusetts in 1871. ('Pragmatism
in Retrospect: A Last Formulation' (1906), *Philosophical Writings of Peirce*,
p. 269.) This was a place described by the novelist Henry James, William's
brother, as somewhere William and 'various other long-headed youths . . .
wrangle grimly and stick to the question. It gives me a headache merely to
know of it' (John Murphy, *Pragmatism From Peirce to Davidson*, Westview
Press, Boulder, San Francisco, Oxford, 1990, p. 15). This is perhaps not
uncharacteristic of the image of philosophers in literary culture prior to Derrida:
we wrangle grimly. It may explain something of Derrida's success in the USA:
Derrida wrangles gaily. Later, Peirce attempted to distinguish his position from
James's by adopting the term 'pragmaticism', which he reckoned 'ugly enough
to be safe from kidnappers'. Ugly enough, in fact, to have escaped use. I shall
thus continue to use the more familiar 'pragmatism', with the modification
'Peircian' or 'metaphysical' where necessary.

18 'The Essentials of Pragmatism', *Philosophical Writings*, p. 252.

19 See Jürgen Habermas, 'Peirce's Logic of Inquiry: The Dilemma of a Scholastic
Realism Restored by the Logic of Language', in *Knowledge and Human
Interests*, pp. 91–112; and Karl-Otto Apel, 'Transcendental Semiotics and

Truth: The Relevance of a Peircean Consensus Theory of Truth in the Present Debate about Truth Theories', in his *From a Transcendental-Semiotic Point of View*, edited by Marianna Papastephanou, Manchester University Press, Manchester, 1998, pp. 64–80.

Considerable confusion is generated by the failure to distinguish between epistemic theories of 'truth' of the Habermasian–Apelian variety (which are about the conditions under which *statements* may justifiably be *held* to be true) and more classical ontological theories (which are about what truth 'is'). The former are premised on the rejection of the classical distinction between truth and knowledge which the latter presuppose. Apel and Habermas convert Peirce's logic of inquiry into a 'theory of truth' by discarding Peirce's realism, but it is confusing to designate this theory 'Peircean' since it is in direct opposition to Peirce's views about truth. Proponents of epistemic theories tend to assume that nobody holds ontological theories 'these days'. But it is the ontological dimension which imparts practical significance to theory.

Peirce is a metaphysical pragmatist. However, the distinction between metaphysical and non-metaphysical pragmatism is not internal to pragmatism itself, but rather concerns views which are held alongside it. According to Peirce, 'pragmatism is, in itself, no doctrine of metaphysics, no attempt to determine any truth of things. It is merely of a method of ascertaining the meanings of hard words and abstract concepts. ... As to the ulterior and indirect effects of practising the pragmatist method, that is quite another affair', 'Pragmatism in Retrospect', *Philosophical Writings*, p. 271. It was this 'other affair', Peirce thought, on which he differed from James and other pragmatists.

More recently, Habermas appears to have gone some way towards acknowledging the ontological dimension to the concept of truth, in two ways. First, following Putnam's critique of Rorty, he writes that: 'all languages offer the possibility of distinguishing between what is true and what we hold to be true. The *supposition* of a common objective world is built into the pragmatics of every single linguistic usage', *Postmetaphysical Thinking*, p. 138. And second, in his turn to a Heideggerian conception of world-disclosure in his views about art. Indeed, he accuses Peirce of neglecting the 'world-disclosing function of the sign' apparent in the invention of new vocabularies. 'Peirce and Communication' (1989, in ibid., p. 106). However, in the first case, the apparent commitment to realism is metacritically transformed back into a transcendental condition of communication, and hence a *mere* supposition. Although there is still some ambivalence about this: 'The moment of unconditionality that is preserved in the discursive concepts of a fallibilistic truth and morality is not an absolute, or it is at most an absolute that has become fluid as a critical procedure', ibid., p. 144. An absolute that has become fluid as a critical procedure ... The reason for this is that unlike Peirce's speculative 'final opinion', for Habermas, the transcendentally implicit rational ideal is 'unattainable'. The 'constraint of reality' is thus *wholly* negative: reality 'impose[s] restrictions on our knowledge ... only in such a way that it rejects false opinions when our interpretations founder upon it', ibid., p. 96. In fact, it is 'not even stable enough for a negative metaphysics' since 'that continues to offer an equivalent for the extra-mundane perspective of a God's-eye view', ibid., pp. 144–5. However, it is not entirely clear what is wrong with this if it's 'a supposition built into the pragmatics of every single linguistic usage'. The Popperian attempt to render the reality-constraint wholly negative thus takes us back to Putnam's objection to Rorty's radical contextualism (an objection which is itself of a Peircean kind): namely, how, then, are we to give content to the idea of *learning*, to an *improvement* in our standards of rationality? This is only possible if we hypothetically project a 'final opinion' as an *historical* event.

In the second case, the differentiation of value-spheres deprives art of both cognitive and moral-practical significance, rendering its 'disclosures' purely aesthetic. This is inconsistent with the experience of art. The attempt to confine world-disclosure to the aesthetic appears increasingly artificial and implausible, threatening the whole Habermasian paradigm with a Heideggerian destruction. It is symptomatic of Habermas's difficulties here that at the very moment of discarding the ontological dimension of Peirce's thought in favour of methodologism, Habermas inconsistently retained the notion of disclosure: 'From this transcendental perspective it is not meaningful to talk in the language of Scholastic realism about the existence of the universal. Rather, within the framework posited with the process of inquiry we constitute the objects of possible experience such that reality is disclosed in a definite constellation of the universal and the particular. This constellation can be demonstrated in the modes of inference on which the process of inquiry depends', 'Peirce's Logic of Inquiry', p. 112. The question is: what ensures that the modes of inference which constitute the logic of inquiry 'disclose' an independently existing world? One can detect in the Adornean language of 'a definite constellation of the universal and the particular' the influence of Adorno's anti-Heideggerian aversion to the *language* of 'ontology' upon Habermas's very unAdornean methodologism. It is ironic that the ultimate consequence of the undialectical rejection of ontolgy here should be its return in an explicitly Heideggerian form. The early Heidegger has, of course, at times been read in the USA as a pragmatist (as have more or less all the main figures in the post-Kantian European tradition). However, the least one can say is that if the early Heidegger is a pragmatist, he is a 'metaphysical' one, albeit it in a radically different way from Peirce.

20 William James, *Pragmatism*, Hackett, Indianapolis, 1981, pp. 30 and 37 – emphases added; John J. McDermott, (ed.), *The Writings of William James*, Chicago University Press, Chicago and London, 1977, p. 360.

21 See, for example, Christopher Hookway, 'Logical Principles and Philosophical Attitudes: Peirce's Response to James's Pragmatism' and Hilary Putnam, 'James's Theory of Truth', in Ruth Anna Putnam (ed.), *The Cambridge Companion to William James*, Cambridge University Press, Cambridge, 1997, pp. 145–65 and 166–87. Both essays seek to complicate the relationship between Peirce's and James's positions, but each ends up confirming the established differences, with relatively minor qualifications.

22 James, *Pragmatism*, p. 27.

23 See Jacques Rancière, *Disagreement: Politics and Philosophy*, trans. Julie Rose, Minnesota University Press, Minneapolis and London, 1999.

24 Richard Rorty, 'Postmodern Bourgeois Liberalism', in his *Objectivity, Relativism and Truth: Philosophical Papers, Vol. 1*, Cambridge University Press, Cambridge, 1991, pp. 197–202.

25 For the diagnosis of this dual reduction as the orientating structure of Stuart Hall's work, see Mulhern, *Culture/Metaculture*, pp. 127–9. Within cultural theory, it was Ernesto Laclau and Chantal Mouffe's semiotic reception of Althusser's modification of Gramsci's conception of conjuncture which proved decisive; Laclau and Mouffe, *Hegemony and Socialist Strategy: Towards a Democratic Politics*, Verso, London and New York, 1985. The Nietzschean dimension to this conception of contingency has been brought out by the subsequent importation of a deconstructive conception of the performative, popularized by Judith Butler.

Performativity, according to Butler, is 'that aspect of discourse that has the capacity to produce what it names . . . through a certain kind of repetition and recitation . . . the discursive mode by which ontological effects are installed'. Peter Osborne and Lynne Segal, 'Gender as Peformance: An Interview with Judith Butler', in P. Osborne (ed.), *A Critical Sense: Interviews with Intellectuals*, Routledge, London and New York, 1996, p. 112. See also Mulhern's review of the English translation of Althusser's *Machiavelli and Us*, 'Althusser and Us', *Radical Philosophy*, 101 (May/June 2000), pp. 39–42.

26 Friedrich Nietzsche, 'Uses and Disadvantages of History for Life' in his *Untimely Meditations*, trans. R.J. Hollingdale, Cambridge University Press, Cambridge, 1997, pp. 57–124. In Nietzsche's later work, this epistemological indifference acquires a cosmological cast in the theory of eternal recurrence, but this is a metaphysical – indeed mythic – implication which cultural theory has yet to confront; except incidentally, perhaps, in its darker, more self-destructively Deleuzean moments.

27 Walter Benjamin, 'Convolute N [On the Theory of Knowledge, Theory of Progress]', [N11, 3]; *The Arcades Project*, trans. Howard Eiland and Kevin McLaughlin, Harvard University Press, Cambridge, MA, 1999, p. 476.

28 See Nietzsche, 'On Truth and Lying in a Non-Moral Sense', in Friedrich Nietzsche, *The Birth of Tragedy and Other Writings*, trans. Ronald Spiers, Cambridge University Press, Cambridge, 1999, pp. 139–53. This is also a source of Habermas's pragmatism, which attempts to be neither Nietzschean nor metaphysical. See *Knowledge and Human Interests*, ch. 12.

29 'Truth and Truths/Knowledge and Elements of Knowledge' (1920–21), in Walter Benjamin, *Selected Writings, Volume One, 1913–1926*, Harvard University Press, Cambridge, MA, 1997, pp. 278–9. This quotation sums up Benjamin's principled anti-Hegelianism. Cf. Walter Benjamin, *The Origin of German Tragic Drama* (1925), trans. John Osborne, New Left Books, London, 1977, pp. 27–36.

30 'The correctness of a piece of knowledge is never identical with its truth, but every correct assertion has a relation with the truth', ibid., p. 279. In this early fragment, Benjamin follows the Romantics in maintaining that 'truths . . . can be expressed . . . only in art.' Later, he generalized the model to the experience of all cultural objects and practices, by treating them as metaphysically equivalent to art. The eschatological dimension of totality here derives, famously, from Benjamin's reception of a particular Judaic tradition, which he subjected to a secular political 'refunctioning'. However, without a direct philosophical defence, this refunctioning is in danger of being relativized to the cultural remnants of the Judaic-Christian tradition. For a reconstruction of the conceptual logic of the secular version, and its defence on the basis of the extension of an early Heideggerian conception of being-towards-death (death is the material meaning of messianic exteriority), see *The Politics of Time*, ch. 4.

31 Cf. Peter Osborne, 'Small-scale Victories, Large-scale Defeats: Walter Benjamin's Politics of Time', in Andrew Benjamin and Peter Osborne (eds.), *Walter Benjamin's Philosophy: Destruction and Experience*, Routledge, London and New York, 1994; 2nd edition, Clinamen Press, Manchester, 2000, p. 87; *The Politics of Time*, p. 147. The semiotic dimension of this metaphysical investment in the image is discussed in the next chapter.

32 Cf. Howard Caygill, *Walter Benjamin: The Colour of Experience*, Routledge, London and New York, 1998, p. 26.

33 Walter Benjamin, *The Origin of German Tragic Drama*, trans. John Osborne, New Left Books, London, 1977, p. 36.

34 *The Arcades Project* [N11, 3], p. 476.

35 Ibid., [K1, 2], pp. 388–9.
36 *Selected Writings*, Vol. 1, p. 185.
37 Adorno, 'Why Still Philosophy?', p. 17.
38 Osborne, *The Politics of Time*, ch. 2, especially pp. 52–62.
39 See John Kraniauskas, 'Globalization is Ordinary: The Transnationalization of Cultural Studies', *Radical Philosophy* 90 (July-August 1998), pp. 9–19.
40 Paul Gilroy, *The Black Atlantic: Modernity and Double Consciousness*, Verso, London, 1993.
41 Cf. Gayatri Spivak's description of cultural politics as 'that area that engages in coding subject-production', 'Who Claims Alterity?', in Barbara Kruger and Phil Mariani (eds.), *Remaking History*, Dia Art Foundation Discussions in Contemporary Culture no. 4, Bay Press, Seattle, 1989, p. 275. It is important to distinguish this from the *reduction* of culture to signification: coding subject-production always involves more than just coding. It is symptomatic of the increasing displacement of the notion of culture by that of subjectivity that in the recent exchange between Judith Butler and Nancy Fraser over the 'merely cultural' neither hazarded a definition or even a rough description of 'the cultural'. Judith Butler, 'Merely Cultural' and Nancy Fraser, 'Heterosexism, Misrecognition and Capitalism: A Response to Judith Butler', *Social Text* 52–53 (1997), pp. 265–78 and 279–89.
42 Karl Marx, *Grundrisse*, trans. Martin Nicholaus, Penguin Books in association with New Left Review, Harmondsworth, 1973, Introduction (1857), p. 105. It is notable the extent to which Marx's views on abstraction had developed in the decade since *The German Ideology*, where abstractions were seen to be able 'only to serve to facilitate the arrangement of historical material, to indicate the sequence of its separate strata', Marx/Engels, *Collected Works*, 5, p. 37. Subsequently, the idea of 'summing up the most general results' of the positive sciences would become concretized as the problem of dialectical presentation, the order of which is to be distinguished from the order of research. See Marx's 'Afterword to the 2nd German edition of *Capital*' (1873), Karl Marx, *Capital: A Critique of Political Economy*, Volume 1, trans. Samuel Moore and Edward Aveling, Lawrence and Wishart, London, 1954, p. 28.
43 *Hegel's Science of Logic*, trans. A.V. Miller, Humanities Press, Atlantic Highlands, 1989, p. 59.

2 SIGN AND IMAGE

1 Cf. 'Culture and Power: An Interview with Stuart Hall', pp. 24–5. Roland Barthes' *Mythologies* (1957) first appeared in English translation in 1972, the same year as Foucault's *The Archaeology of Knowledge* (1969). Derrida's *Of Grammatology* (1967) followed four years later, in 1976. By this time Barthes himself had moved on to the more fluid model of textuality summed up in 'From Work to Text' (1971, translated in Roland Barthes, *Image–Music–Text*, Fontana/Collins, 1977, pp. 155–64), a move he reflected on in 'Change the Object Itself: Myth Today' (1972, in ibid., pp. 165–9). In this respect, the reception of structuralist and post-structuralist semiotics into English-language cultural theory occurred at more or less the same time.
2 'Logic as Semiotic: The Theory of Signs', *Philosophical Writings of Peirce*, p. 105.
3 Much of this work originated in studies of the psychology of perception. See, for example, Ernst Gombrich, *Art and Illusion: A Study in the Psychology of Pictorial Representation*, Phaidon, London, 1960; James J. Gibson, *The Senses*

Considered as Perceptual Systems, Unwin and Allen, London, 1968. During the 1960s, Peirce's reputation was further disadvantaged by the narrowly behaviourist interpretation of his work offered by his main follower, Charles Morris, in *Signs, Language and Behavior*, Prentice-Hall, New York, 1946.

4 For the distinction between arbitrary and motivated signs, see Roland Barthes, *Elements of Semiology* (1964), trans., Annette Lavers and Colin Smith, Hill and Wang, New York, 1973, pp. 50–4. This translation first appeared in 1967, but it was the subsequent reception of *Mythologies* that secured it a broader readership.

5 Barthes, 'From Work to Text', p. 164. More generally, see John Mowitt, *Text: The Genealogy of an Antidisciplinary Object*, Duke University Press, Durham, 1993.

6 See Kaja Silverman, *The Subject of Semiotics*, Oxford University Press, New York and Oxford, 1983.

7 See in particular, Laclau and Mouffe, 'Beyond the Positivity of the Social: Antagonisms and Hegemony', *Hegemony and Socialist Strategy*, ch. 3. For a retrospective view on this sequence of theoretical layerings, see Hall, 'Culture and Power', pp. 25–36.

8 Homi K. Bhabha, *The Location of Culture*, Routledge, London and New York, 1994; Judith Butler, *The Psychic Life of Power: Theories of Subjection*, Stanford University Press, Stanford, 1997.

9 See Emile Benveniste, *Problems in General Linguistics*, trans. Mary Elizabeth Meek, University of Miami Press, Coral Gables, 1971.

10 See, for example, the introductory sections on 'culture' in Paul du Gay *et al.*, *Doing Cultural Studies: The Story of the Sony Walkman*, Sage/Open University, London, Thousand Oaks, CA, and New Delhi, 1997, pp. 11–24 – the first in a six volume series on Culture, Media and Identities. That deconstruction remains within this structure, for all its criticisms of it, is a distinctive feature of its methodological purism. As Derrida put it: 'the proper space of a grammatology is at the same time opened and closed by *The Course in General Linguistics*', Jacques Derrida, *Of Grammatology*, trans. Gayatri Chakravorty Spivak, Johns Hopkins University Press, Baltimore and London, 1976, p. 58.

11 Peter Osborne, 'Radicalism Without Limit: Discourse, Democracy and the Politics of Identity', in Peter Osborne (ed.), *Socialism and the Limits of Liberalism*, Verso, London and New York, 1991, pp. 201–25. See also Butler's definition of performativity quoted in note 25 to ch. 1, above.

12 For some reflections on the Laplanchean alternative to Lacan and Kristeva here, see Osborne, *The Politics of Time*, pp. 98–112, and, with particular reference to the issue of generalization, ch. 7, below.

13 See in particular, Peter Wollen, 'The Semiology of the Cinema', in his *Signs and Meaning in the Cinema* (1969), 4th ed., British Film Institute, London, 1998, pp. 79–106, and the 'Conclusion', added to the 2nd edition (1972), pp. 107–18; David Osmond-Smith, 'The Iconic Process in Musical Communication' *VS* 3, 1972 and 'Formal Iconism in Music', *VS* 5, 1973; Teresa de Lauretis, 'Imaging' and 'Semiotics and Experience', in her *Alice Doesn't: Feminism, Semiotics, Cinema*, Indiana University Press, Bloomington, 1982, pp. 37–69 and 158–86 and 'The Rhetoric of Violence: Considerations on Representation and Gender', in her *Technologies of Gender: Essays in Theory, Film, and Fiction*, Macmillan, Basingstoke, 1987, pp. 31–50; Margaret Iversen, 'Saussure versus Peirce: Models for a Semiotics of Visual Art', in A.L. Rees and F. Borzello (eds.), *The New Art History*, Camden Press, London, 1986, pp. 82–93. The inspirations behind these successive turns to Peirce were Roman Jakobson, Umberto Eco, and Meyer Schapiro, respectively.

For a critique of Wollen's collapse back into Saussureanism, already evident in the 1972 'Conclusion' to *Signs and Meaning in the Cinema,* see D.N. Roderick, *The Crisis of Political Modernism: Criticism and Ideology in Contemporary Film* (1988), 2nd ed., University of California Press, Berkeley, 1994, chs. 2 and 6. Like others interested in the articulation of semiotics with psychoanalysis, Wollen came to associate the icon with the Lacanian imaginary, thereby performing a psychoanalytical reduction of its non-linguistic aspect that removed it from the context of Peirce's pragmatism. Psychoanalysis has also inhibited de Lauretis – a more consistent Peircean – from further developing the framework sketched in her 'Semiotics and Experience'. What follows below is a mediated return to the perspective opened up by that essay.

14 Umberto Eco, 'Peirce and the Semiotic Foundations of Openness: Signs as Texts and Texts as Signs' (1976), in his *The Role of the Reader: Explorations in the Semiotics of Texts,* Indiana University Press, Bloomington, 1984, pp. 175–99; here, pp. 176, 194 and 196. The notion of the interpretant, Eco claims, 'saves the category of content (and of meaning) from being an ungraspable platonic abstraction or an undetectable mental event', p. 197.

15 Umberto Eco, *A Theory of Semiotics,* Indiana University Press, Bloomington, 1976, pp. 8–9.

16 Ibid., p. 16. Cf. Peirce's famous definition of 1897: 'A sign, or *representamen,* is something which stands to somebody for something in some respect or capacity', *Philosophical Writings,* p. 99; or St Augustine's: 'A sign is something which, in addition to the substance absorbed by the senses, calls to mind of itself some other thing.' Quoted by Barthes, *Elements of Semiology,* p. 100, ft. 29.

17 *A Theory of Semiotics,* pp. 191, 49.

18 Ibid., pp. 191, 121. Cf. Barthes' remarks on the limiting function of the principle of relevance that defines the field of semiological research, *Elements of Semiology,* pp. 95–8.

19 'Peirce and the Semiotic Foundations of Openness', p. 179.

20 'Critique of Iconism', *A Theory of Semiotics,* pp. 191–217. The quotations are from pp. 193, 195, 199, 203, 213, 216 respectively.

21 Barthes, 'The Photographic Message' (1961), in *Image-Music-Text,* p. 17.

22 Pierce, *Philosophical Writings,* pp. 106, 119.

23 *A Theory of Semiotics,* p. 116.

24 Pierce, *Philosophical Writings,* p. 99. As Eco emphasizes ('Peirce and the Semiotic Foundations of Openness', p. 180), the Interpretant, or Third, must thus be another sign, opening up the prospect of an unlimited semiosis or chain of interpretants.

25 Ibid., p. 104.

26 Ibid., pp. 104–5.

27 André Bazin, 'The Ontology of the Photographic Image' (1945), in his *What is Cinema? Volume 1,* trans., Hugh Gray, University of California Press, Berkeley, 1967, pp. 9–19, here pp. 15–16.

28 Willard Van Orman Quine, *From a Logical Point of View: Logico-Philosophical Essays,* Harvard University Press, Cambridge, MA, 1953.

29 David Hume, 'Of the Standard of Taste' (1757), in his *Selected Essays,* Oxford University Press World Classics, Oxford, 1993, pp. 133–53. It was this kind of analytically updated Humeanism which provided the philosophical basis for the strong anti-aesthetic programme in conceptual art, epitomized by Kosuth's predilection for the work of A.J. Ayer. See ch. 6, below.

30 J.O. Urmson and Jonathan Rée, *The Concise Encyclopaedia of Western Philosophy and Philosophers,* Unwin Hyman, London, 2nd ed., 1989, p. 3.

31 Immanuel Kant, *Critique of Pure Reason*, trans. Norman Kemp-Smith, MacMillan, London and Basingstoke, 1933, A19–49, B33–73. See Gilles Deleuze, *Kant's Critical Philosophy*, trans. Hugh Tomlinson and Barbara Habberjam, Athlone Press, London, 1984. As Deleuze points out, the unity of this relational totality is in fact more that of a 'fundamental discord' than a harmony. See also, Deleuze's reading of the fracturing of the 'I' by time in Kant's *Critique of Pure Reason* in his *Difference and Repetition*, trans. Paul Patton, Athlone Press, London, 1994, pp. 85–7. This fracturing is a fracturing of the 'I' between its inward and outward references (transcendental 'I' as grammatical subject of utterance and passive self). The metaphorics of 'inner' and 'outer' in Kant interpretation is complicated by Kant's use of the terms to refer to space and time, respectively, although time has both 'inward' and 'outward' reference in the sense adopted here.

32 Cf. Christoph Menke, *The Sovereignty of Art: Aesthetic Negativity in Adorno and Derrida*, trans. Neil Solomon, MIT Press, Cambridge, MA, 1998, ch. 2, in which Menke offers a semiotic interpretation of aesthetic negativity.

33 Kant, *Critique of Judgement*, pp. 217, 215, 44, 62.

34 *The Sovereignty of Art*, p. 34.

35 Ibid., pp. 36–7.

36 *A Theory of Semiotics*, pp. 13, 261, 266, 262, 266, 267.

37 Cf. Kant, *Critique of Pure Reason*, A113: 'The ground of the possibility of the association of the manifold, so far as it lies in the object, is named the affinity of the manifold.'

38 Aristotle, *De Anima*, III 7.431a.

39 See Mitchell, 'What is an Image?' in his *Iconology: Image, Text, Ideology*, Chicago University Press, Chicago, 1986, pp. 7–46.

40 See Hans Belting, *Likeness and Presence: A History of the Image Before the Age of Art*, Chicago University Press, Chicago, 1994.

41 'The Ontology of the Photographic Image', p. 14.

42 Roland Barthes, *Camera Lucida: Reflections on Photography* (1980), trans. Richard Howard, Fontana, London, 1984, pp. 76–7, 91.

43 Siegfried Kracauer, 'Photography' (1927), in his *The Mass Ornament: Weimar Essays*, trans. Thomas Y. Levin, Harvard University Press, Cambridge, MA, 1995, pp. 47–63; here, pp. 62, 50–1, 52, 55, 58, 49, 59, 62–3.

44 Barthes, 'Rhetoric of the Image', in *Image-Music-Text*, p. 44.

45 *Camera Lucida*, pp. 87–9, 113.

46 Ibid., pp. 27, 30, 82, 45, 49; Kracauer, 'Photography', pp. 54, 51. For an historical account of photography's dialectical relation to the everyday, see John Roberts, *The Art of Interruption: Realism, Photography and the Everyday*, Manchester University Press, Manchester, 1998. There is a danger in Barthes' account of the *punctum* of the reduction of photography to a particular (highly personalized) sub-genre: the snapshot/family album. However, I believe the analysis is generalizable beyond this aspect of his account, although it may lead to different readings of particular images.

47 *Camera Lucida*, pp. 4, 30, 91, 49, 94, 119, 96, 88.

48 An 'unruly desire to know', 'the tiny spark of contingency . . . with which reality has so to speak seared the subject', 'the inconspicuous spot', 'the physiognomic aspects of visual worlds which dwell in the smallest things', 'a present which is not in transition, but in which time stands still', 'to blast open the continuum of history', 'a memory as it flashes up at a moment of danger', 'every presentation of history [must] begin with awakening; in fact, it should treat of nothing else', 'the angel of history . . . sees one single catastrophe', 'a

magical value', Walter Benjamin, 'A Small History of Photography', in his *One-Way Street and Other Essays,* trans. Edmund Jephcott and Kingsley Shorter, New Left Books, London, 1979, pp. 242–3; 'Theses on the Philosophy of History', in *Illuminations,* trans. Harry Zohn, Fontana, London, 1973, pp. 264, 257; 'Convolute N', *The Arcades Project,* p. 464 [N4, 3]; 'Theses', p. 259; 'A Small History', p. 243, respectively.

49 *Camera Lucida,* pp. 96–7.

50 'A Small History', p. 243.

51 The difference, perhaps, between a Christian and a Judaic sense of history? Barthes explicitly links the photograph to resurrection – 'might we not say of it what the Byzantines said of the image of Christ which impregnated St Veronica's napkin: it was not made by the hand of man, *acheiropoietos?'* (*Camera Lucida,* p. 82) – whereas for Benjamin the perspective of redemption was either one outside of time or within nature. See, for example, his 'Theologico-Political Fragment' (1921), *One-Way Street,* pp. 155–6. The politics of *Camera Lucida,* such as there is one, is a personalism of private space.

52 *Camera Lucida,* p. 32.

53 'A Small History', pp. 243, 250–3; 'The Work of Art in the Age of Mechanical Reproduction' (1939), in *Illuminations,* pp. 219–53.

54 *Camera Lucida,* pp. 8, 18, 71.

55 Roland Barthes, *Roland Barthes* (1975), trans. Richard Howard, Macmillan, Basingstoke, 1977, pp. 46, 3–4, 44. For a critique of the growing obsession with singularity in post-war French thought, apparent in Derrida's essay on Barthes ('The Deaths of Roland Barthes', in Hugh J. Silverman (ed.), *Philosophy and Non-Philosophy since Merleau-Ponty,* Routledge, New York, 1988, pp. 259–96), see Peter Hallward, 'The Singular and the Specific: Recent French Philosophy', *Radical Philosophy* 99 (Jan/February 2000), pp. 6–18.

56 With the exception of polaroids, although these are, of course, amenable to further photographic reproduction, like everything else. Photographs of photographs (half-tones) are the staple of media imagery.

57 *The Arcades Project,* [N3, 1], p. 462.

58 Theodor W. Adorno, *Aesthetic Theory,* trans. Robert Hullot Kentor, Minnesota University Press, Minneapolis, 1997, p. 33.

59 For a discussion of the replicability of sign vehicles as a condition of signification, see Eco, *A Theory of Semiotics,* pp. 178–83. Photographs are icons of their referents but 'doubles' (that is, absolute replicas) of each other, if printed from the same negative.

60 See Caygill, *The Colour of Experience,* ch. 3.

61 *A Theory of Semiotics,* pp. 222–3.

62 Ibid., pp. 49 and 191. Cf. p. 25, above.

63 Ibid., p. 121. Cf. p. 25, above.

64 Peirce, 'Pragmatism in Retrospect', pp. 275, 277, 274; Eco, 'Peirce and the Semiotic Foundations of Openness', pp. 180–91, especially p. 189; Derrida, *Of Grammatology,* p. 49.

65 Peirce, quoted by Eco, 'Peirce and the Semiotic Foundations of Openness', p. 189.

66 Peirce, 'Pragmatism in Retrospect', pp. 277, 283, 286.

67 'Peirce and the Semiotic Foundations of Openness', pp. 195, 194.

68 'Pragmatism in Retrospect', pp. 277–8. 'It is noticeable that the iteration of the action is often said to be indispensable to the formation of a habit; but a very moderate exercise of observation suffices to refute this error.'

69 De Lauretis, 'Semiotics and Experience', pp. 178, 183, 179.

70 'Pragmatism in Retrospect', pp. 280–1; emphases added. Cf. Peirce's notion of truth: 'truth's independence of individual opinions is due (so far as there is any "truth") to its being the predestined result to which sufficient inquiry *would* ultimately lead', ibid., p. 288.

71 Despite his insistence on a dialectical relationship between realism and pragmatism in Peirce's work, Eco describes Peirce's position as 'not an ontological, but a pragmatic realism', thereby undermining the basis for any such dialectic. ('Peirce and the Semiotic Foundations of Openness', p. 193.) It is unclear how pragmatism can be a realism of any sort without an ontological dimension (see note 17 to ch. 1, above); not least with regard to the subject. That such realism is a realism of 'result' not 'datum' (Eco, ibid., p. 192) makes it no less ontological. Subjectivity is practical being. The ontological aspect of Peirce's realism is clear in his distinction between the 'immediate' and the 'dynamic' object. The dynamic object is the referent; the immediate objects, the way in which the dynamic object is 'focused' or represented by a sign. Ontologically, it is subjects' practical relations to other dynamic objects which determine the use of signs; epistemologically, we only have access to dynamic objects via immediate objects. The self is as much a product of inference as any other dynamic object. Cf. Deleuze's account of the relationship between the 'I' and the passive self in *Difference and Repetition*, cited in note 31, above.

72 Benjamin, 'The Work of Art in the Age of Mechanical Reproduction', p. 242; Caygill, *The Colour of Experience*, p. 115. Benjamin is referring to architecture. For Peirce, perceptual judgements are themselves forms of logical inference: 'extreme' forms of abduction.

73 Barthes, *Elements of Semiology*, p. 98.

74 Benjamin, *The Arcades Project*, [N3, 1], p. 462–3.

75 Ibid., p. 463.

76 I use the expression 'photographic image' here in its most generic technical sense, including film and television. For an application of this idea to an analysis of the historical significance of the work of the German photo-painter Gerhard Richter, see my 'Painting Negation: Gerhard Richter's Negatives', *October* 62 (Fall 1992), pp. 103–14 and 'Abstract Images: Sign, Image and Aesthetic in the Paintings of Gerhard Richter', forthcoming in *Le Part de l'Œil*, Vol. 17 (2000).

77 See, for example, Lawrence Grossberg, 'Experience, Signification, and Reality: The Boundaries of Cultural Semiotics' (1982), in his *Bringing It All Back Home: Essays on Cultural Studies*, Duke University Press, Durham and London, 1997, pp. 70–102, and, more recently, 'Cultural Studies, Modern Logics, and Theories of Globalization', in Angela McRobbie (ed.), *Back to Reality? Social Experience and Cultural Studies*, Manchester University Press, Manchester, 1997, pp. 7–35. Grossberg is the editor of the journal *Cultural Studies*.

78 Gilles Deleuze and Félix Guattari, *A Thousand Plateaus: Capitalism and Schizophrenia* (1980), trans. Brian Massumi, University of Minnesota Press, Minneapolis, 1987, ch. 5, '587 B.C.–A.D. 70: On Several Regimes of Signs'. I use the name 'Deleuze' here to include the joint authorship with Guattari, in order to emphasize the latter's theoretical continuity with both Deleuze's earlier works on the history of philosophy and the subsequent philosophical texts written in Deleuze's 'own voice'.

79 Certainly, Caygill's recent Benjamin is proto-Deleuzean. Caygill's reading eliminates the messianic dimension of Benjamin's thought in favour of the speculative chromatism of his early writings, in which the 'intensive infinity of colour' displaces 'the extensive infinity of form'. (*The Colour of Experience*, p. 83.) Cf. Deleuze's vision of a 'chromatic linguistics': 'All languages . . . in

immanent continuous variation: neither synchrony nor diachrony, but asynchrony, chromaticism as a variable and continuous state of language', Deleuze and Guattari, *A Thousand Plateaus*, p. 97.

80 Gilles Deleuze and Félix Guattari, *Anti-Oedipus: Capitalism and Schizophrenia* (1972), trans. Robert Hurley, Mark Seam, and Helen R. Lane, University of Minnesota Press, Minneapolis, 1983, pp. 26–7.

81 Ibid., p. 380.

82 *A Thousand Plateaus*, p. 531, note 41; Gilles Deleuze, *Cinema 2: The Time-Image* (1985), trans. Hugh Tomlinson and Robert Galeta, Athlone Press, London, 1989, p. 30; *A Thousand Plateaus*, p. 148; *Cinema 2*, pp. 28–9.

83 *A Thousand Plateaus*, pp. 141–2.

84 *Anti-Oedipus*, pp. 139, 142, 4–6, 36, 42, 39.

85 *A Thousand Plateaus*, pp. 90, 88; *Anti-Oedipus*, pp. 372, 374, 376.

86 *A Thousand Plateaus*, pp. 531 (note 41), 112, 142.

87 *Anti-Oedipus*, pp. 321, 367, 321–2, 373.

88 *A Thousand Plateaus*, pp. 142–6. See also 'Conclusion: Concrete Rules and Abstract Machines', ibid., pp. 501–14, which is actually more of a glossary.

89 'Pragmatics as a whole would consist in this: [i] making a *tracing* of the mixed semiotics, under the generative component; [ii] making the transformational *map* of the regimes, with their possibilities for translation and creation, for budding along the lines of the tracings; [iii] making the *diagram* of the abstract machines that are in play in each case, either as potentialities or as effective emergences; [iv] outlining the *program* of the assemblages that distribute everything and bring a circulation of movement with alternatives, jumps, and mutations', ibid., pp. 146–7.

90 Gilles Deleuze, *Cinema 1: The Movement-Image* (1983), trans. Hugh Tomlinson and Barbara Habberjam, Athlone Press, London, 1986, pp. 98–9, 197–8.

91 Ibid., p. 96. Cf. Bazin's definition of the photographic image – 'the object itself ... freed from the conditions of time and space' – note 27, above.

92 Ibid., p. 200.

93 Deleuze, *Difference and Repetition*, p. 74. Cf. Gilles Deleuze, *Bergsonism* (1966), trans. Hugh Tomlinson and Barbara Habberjam, Zone Books, New York, 1991, p. 53.

94 For example, Grossberg, *Bringing it All Back Home*, pp. 4–5.

95 Michael Hardt and Antonio Negri, *Empire*, Harvard University Press, Cambridge, MA and London, 2000, p. 28.

96 Deleuze and Guattari, *A Thousand Plateaus*, p. 505. Cf. Peter Hallward, 'Deleuze and the Redemption from Interest', *Radical Philosophy* 81 (Jan/Feb 1997), pp. 6–21. Iain MacKenzie's objection to Hallward that 'Deleuze invokes the Real in order to show how we may create new ways of living, not so that life should be dissolved into one redemptive univocal realm' ('Creativity as Criticism: The Philosophical Constructivism of Deleuze and Guattari', *Radical Philosophy* 86 (Sept/Oct 1998), pp. 7–18, p. 18, note 57) may correctly state Deleuze's motivation, but it fails to engage the criticism at the (ontological) level at which it is pitched.

97 Meaghan Morris, 'A Question of Cultural Studies', in McRobbie (ed.), *Back to Reality?*, p. 54.

98 Gilles Deleuze and Félix Guattari, *What is Philosophy?* (1991), trans. Graham Burchell and Hugh Tomlinson, Verso, London and New York, 1994, Pt 1.

99 Alain Badiou, *Deleuze: The Clamour of Being* (1997), trans. Louise Burchill, University of Minnesota Press, Minneapolis, 2000. Cf. Alain Badiou, *Manifesto for Philosophy* (1989), trans. Norman Madarasz, University of Minnesota Press, Minneapolis, 1999.

100 See ch. 7, below.
101 Gilles Deleuze and Félix Guattari, *Kafka: Towards a Minor Literature* (1975), trans. Dana Polan, University of Minnesota Press, Minneapolis, 1986, ch. 3.

3 MODERNISM AS TRANSLATION

1 This question, which projects a resolution to the disciplinary crisis of philosophy through a new relation to the positive sciences, within the culture of modernism, is at least as old as Feuerbach's 'Necessity for a Reform of Philosophy' (1842). But it retains both its urgency and its force. See Ludwig Feuerbach, 'Necessity for a Reform of Philosophy', *The Fiery Brook: Selected Writings of Ludwig Feuerbach*, trans. Zawar Hanfi, Anchor Books, Garden City, NY, 1972, pp. 145–52.
2 See Jean-Luc Nancy, 'Finite History', in his *The Birth to Presence*, trans. Brian Holmes *et al.*, Stanford University Press, Stanford, 1993, pp. 143–66.
3 See Osborne, *The Politics of Time*, ch. 1.
4 James Clifford, *Routes: Travel and Translation in the Late Twentieth Century*, Harvard University Press, Cambridge, MA, 1997, p. 11.
5 As Sakai puts it: 'the untranslatable, or what can never be appropriated by the economy of the translational communication, cannot exist prior to the enunciation of translation. It is translation that gives birth to the untranslatable', Naoki Sakai, *Translation and Subjectivity: On 'Japan' and Cultural Nationalism*, Minnesota University Press, Minneapolis, 1997, p. 14.
6 Walter Benjamin, 'The Task of the Translator', *Illuminations*, pp. 71–2.
7 Ibid., pp. 73, 78, 80.
8 Ibid., p. 77.
9 Jacques Derrida, *Dissemination*, trans. Barbara Johnson, University of Chicago Press, Chicago, 1981. Cf. Andrew Benjamin, *Translation and the Nature of Philosophy*, Routledge, London and New York, 1989, p. 1.
10 Kant, *Critique of Pure Reason*, A19–22, B33–6.
11 Ibid., B178–81.
12 Osborne, *The Politics of Time*, ch. 5.
13 See for example, Malcolm Bradbury and James McFarlane (eds.), *Modernism, 1890–1930*, Penguin, Harmondsworth, 1976; or in the case of art history, the Open University course book by Frascina *et al.*, *Modernity and Modernism: French Painting in the Nineteenth Century* Yale University Press, New Haven and London, 1993, and its companion volume, Paul Wood *et al.*, *Modernism in Dispute: Art Since the Forties*, Yale University Press, New Haven and London, 1993.
14 See, for example, Astradur Eysteinsson, *The Concept of Modernism*, Cornell University Press, Ithaca, 1990; and Steve Giles (ed.), *Theorizing Modernism: Essays in Critical Theory*, Routledge, London and New York, 1993, respectively.
15 See John Kraniauskas, 'Transculturation and the Work of Translation', *Traces: A Multilingual Journal of Cultural Theory*, no. 1 (2000).
16 Alice Yang, 'Modernism and the Chinese Other in Twentieth Century Art Criticism', in her *Why Asia? Contemporary Asian and AsianAmerican Art*; New York University Press, New York and London, 1998, pp. 129–46; Xudong Zhang, *Chinese Modernism in the Era of Reforms: Cultural Fever, Avant-Garde Fiction and the New Chinese Cinema*, Duke University Press, Durham, 1997. The theoretical frameworks of these two works are very different –

T.J. Clark's socialized version of Greenbergian modernism and Jameson's cultural theory, respectively – but the basic tendency is nonetheless the same.

17 I am thinking, in particular, of the history painting campaign of 1960, in which Socialist Realism was introduced into Chinese visual culture as a specific political dictate.

18 For reflection on the use of culture as 'a supplement to the state' in 'the inculcation of a particular mode of subjectivity', in the inhabitants of a particular territory, 'as a prerequisite to participation in the business of the state, even if participation, here, means no more than accepting "being represented" ', see David Lloyd and Paul Thomas, *Culture and the State*, Routledge, New York and London, 1998. The phrases quoted appear on pp. 46-7.

19 Manuel Castells, *The Information Age: Economy, Society and Culture, Volume 1: The Rise of the Network Society,* Blackwell, Oxford, 1996, p. 411.

4 REMEMBER THE FUTURE?

1 Rob Beamish, 'The Making of the Manifesto', in Leo Panitch and Colin Leys (eds.), *Socialist Register 1998. The Communist Manifesto Now*, p. 233.

2 Eric Hobsbawm, *The Age of Revolution*, Weidenfeld & Nicolson, London, 1962; *The Age of Capital*, Weidenfeld & Nicolson, London, 1975.

3 Marshall Berman, *All That's Solid Melts into Air*, Verso, London, 1982, p. 92.

4 G.W.F. Hegel, *Science of Logic, Volume One*, trans. W.H. Johnson and L.G. Struthers, George Allen and Unwin, London, 1929, p. 164.

5 Goethe, *Faust* I, iv: 'grey are all theories/And green alone life's golden tree'. Cf. G.W.F. Hegel, *Philosophy of Right*, trans. T. M. Knox, Oxford University Press, Oxford, 1952, Preface, p. 13.

6 Quotations from the *Manifesto* are taken from Marx/Engels, *Collected Works*, Vol. 5, pp. 477-519. The translation is altered here to amend 'man' to 'men and women', 'people' or 'human' as appropriate, in the spirit of the critique of abstract humanism in *The German Ideology*.

7 Berman, *All That's Solid*, pp. 89, 102.

8 Pp. 57-60, above.

9 Anna Lawton (ed.), *Russian Futurism Through its Manifestoes, 1912-1928*, trans. Anna Lawton and Herbert Eagle, Cornell University Press, Ithaca and London, 1988, pp. 51-2; 'Manifesto of Surrealism' in André Breton, *Manifestos of Surrealism*, trans. Richard Seaver and Helen R. Lane, University of Michigan Press, Ann Arbor, 1972, p. 47.

10 Berman, *All That's Solid*, p. 121.

11 Karl Marx, 'The Poverty of Philosophy' (1847), in Marx/Engels, *Collected Works*, Vol. 6, p. 127.

12 Michel Foucault, 'What is Enlightenment?', in Paul Rabinow (ed.), *The Foucault Reader*, Penguin, Harmondsworth, 1986, p. 40.

13 Karl Marx and Frederick Engels, *Collected Works*, Vol. 38, Lawrence and Wishart, London, 1982, p. 149.

14 Beamish, 'The Making of the Manifesto', p. 237, n. 49.

15 Cf. Paul Thomas, 'Seeing is Believing: Marx's *Manifesto*, Derrida's Apparition', in Panitch and Leys (eds.), *The Communist Manifesto Now*, p. 205. See also, Marjorie Perloff, 'Violence and Precision: The Manifesto as Art Form', in her *The Futurist Moment: Avant-Garde, Avant Guerre, and the Language of Rupture*, Chicago University Press, Chicago and London, 1986, pp. 81-115.

16 Engels, 'Draft of a Communist Confession of Faith', in Marx/Engels, *Collected Works*, Vol. 6, p. 96.

17 Engels, 'Principles of Communism', in ibid., p. 341.

18 Benveniste, *Problems in General Linguistics*, pp. 195–215.

19 *Russian Futurism*, p. 52.

20 Benjamin, *The Arcades Project*, p. 463. Cf. p. 45, above.

21 Benjamin, 'The Concept of Criticism in German Romanticism'(1920), *Selected Writings*, Vol. 1, pp. 185–6, n. 3. Benjamin quotes Frederich Schlegel: 'The revolutionary desire to realize the kingdom of God on earth is the elastic point of progressive civilization and the inception of modern history.' See also Philippe Lacou-Labarthe and Jean-Luc Nancy, *The Literary Absolute: The Theory of Literature in German Romanticism*, trans. Philip Bernard and Cheryl Lester, SUNY, New York, 1988.

22 Benjamin, 'The Author as Producer', in his *Understanding Brecht*, trans. Anna Bostock, New Left Books, London, 1977, p. 89.

23 Benjamin, 'The Work of Art in the Age of Mechanical Reproduction', *Illuminations*, Fontana, London, 1973, p. 239.

24 Ibid.

25 Jacques Rancière, *The Names of History: On the Poetics of Knowledge*, trans. Hassan Melehy, Minnesota University Press, Minneapolis, 1994, pp. 42–75.

26 Tristan Tzara, 'Dada Manifesto' (1918), in his *Seven Dada Manifestos and Lampisteries*, trans. Barbara Wright, Calder Publications, London, 1977, p. 3.

27 Tzara, 'Dada Manifesto on Feeble Love and Bitter Love', ibid., p. 33.

28 Tzara, 'Dada Manifesto', ibid., p. 3.

29 Caygill, *The Colour of Experience*, Routledge, London, 1998, p. 71. Caygill uses the phrase to summarize Benjamin's reading of Döblin's novel, *Berlin Alexanderplatz*.

30 A reprint of Helen MacFarlane's translation of a shortened version of the *Manifesto*, which first appeared in *The Red Republican*, 9 November, 1850, was published by Merlin Press, London, 1966. I owe the recovery of the 'frightful hobgoblin' to Sheila Rowbotham, 'Dear Dr Marx: A Letter from a Socialist Feminist', in Panitch and Leys (eds.), *The Communist Manifesto Now*, p. 1.

31 See Beamish, 'The Making of the Manifesto', ibid., pp. 231–2.

32 Cf. Paul Thomas, 'Seeing is Believing', ibid., pp. 209–10.

33 Andrew Parker, 'What is a (Communist) Author?', paper to the conference 'Social Emancipation: 150 Years After the Communist Manifesto', 17–20 February 1998, Institute of Philosophy, Havana.

34 Kant, *Critique of Judgement*, p. 58. Hannah Arendt insisted that it is here, in the *Critique of Judgement*, that Kant's political philosophy is to be found. See her *Lectures on Kant's Political Philosophy*, University of Chicago Press, Chicago, 1982.

35 Wolfgang Haug, paper to the conference 'Social Emancipation: 150 Years After the Communist Manifesto', 17–20 February 1998, Institute of Philosophy, Havana.

36 *All That is Solid*, p. 122.

37 Jeff Wall, *Dan Graham's Kammerspiel*, Art Metropole, Toronto, 1991, p. 100.

38 Theodor W. Adorno, 'Aspects of Hegel's Philosophy', *Hegel: Three Studies*, trans. Shierry Weber Nicholsen, MIT Press, Cambridge, MA, 1993, p. 1.

39 Etienne Balibar, in Etienne Balibar and Immanuel Wallerstein, *Race, Nation, Class: Ambiguous Identities*, trans. Chris Turner, Verso, London and New York, 1991, p. 8.

40 Hegel, *Jena RealPhilosophie*, quoted in Georg Lukács, *The Young Hegel: Studies in the Relations between Dialectics and Economics*, trans. Rodney Livingstone, Merlin Press, London, 1975, p. 333.

41 Walter Benjamin, 'A Small History of Photography', p. 243. Cf. pp. 38–9, above.

5 TIME AND THE ARTWORK

1 See Jacques Le Goff, *Memory and History*, trans. Steven Rendall and Elizabeth Claman, Columbia University Press, New York, 1992, pp. 51–216.

2 Eric Hobsbawm and Terence Ranger (eds), *The Invention of Tradition*, Cambridge University Press, Cambridge, 1983.

3 Cf. Osborne, 'Small-scale Victories, Large-scale Defeats', pp. 80–82.

4 See Susan Buck-Morss, 'Aesthetics and Anaesthetics: Walter Benjamin's Artwork Essay Reconsidered', *October* 62, Fall 1992, pp. 5–41.

5 See Osborne, *The Politics of Time*, chs. 2, 4 and 5.

6 See Raphael Samuel, *Theatres of Memory. Volume One: Past and Present in Contemporary Culture*, Verso, London and New York, 1994.

7 Le Goff, *Memory and History*, p. 95.

8 Clement Greenberg, 'Avant-Garde and Kitsch', in *The Collected Essays and Criticism, Volume 1: Perceptions and Judgments, 1939–1944*, Chicago University Press, Chicago, 1986, pp. 5–22; and 'Modernist Painting', in *Volume 4: Modernism with a Vengeance, 1957–1969*, Chicago University Press, Chicago, 1993, pp. 85–93.

9 See p. 90, above.

10 Osborne, *The Politics of Time*, p. 14.

11 Homi Bhabha, *The Location of Culture*, Routledge, London and New York, 1994, p. 242. Cf. Osborne, *The Politics of Time*, p. 198.

12 See Clement Greenberg, 'Towards a Newer Laocoon', in *The Collected Essays and Criticism, Volume 1*, pp. 23–37.

13 Ernest Hello, as quoted by Apollinaire in *Apollinaire on Art: Essays and Reviews, 1902–1918*, Da Capo, New York, n.d., p. 420.

14 See, for example, Clement Greenberg, 'Avant-Garde Attitudes: New Art in the Sixties', in *The Collected Essays and Criticism, Vol. 4*, pp. 292–302. Cf. Peter Osborne, 'Mere Ungovernable Taste: Clement Greenberg Reviewed', *Journal of Philosophy and the Visual Arts* 3, Summer 1992.

15 See, for example, Arthus Danto, 'The End of Art', in *The Philosophical Disenfranchisement of Art*, Columbia University Press, New York, 1986, pp. 81–115.

6 CONCEPTUAL ART AND/AS PHILOSOPHY

1 See Pierre Bourdieu, *The Political Ontology of Martin Heidegger* (1988), trans. Peter Collier, Polity Press, Cambridge, 1991, ch. 2, 'The Philosophical Field and the Space of Possibilities'.

2 See Danto, 'The Philosophical Disenfranchisement of Art', in *The Philosophical Disenfranchisement of Art*, ch. 1.

3 See, for example, Michael Newman, 'Conceptual Art from the 1960s to the 1990s: An Unfinished Project?', *Kunst & Museum Journal*, vol. 7, nos 1–3, 1996, pp. 95–104; John Roberts, 'Photography, Iconophobia and the Ruins of Conceptual Art', in *The Impossible Document: Photography and Conceptual Art in Britain, 1966–1976*, Camerawork, London, 1997, pp. 7–45.

4 Cf. Joseph Kosuth, 'Art After Philosophy', in his *Art After Philosophy and After: Collected Writings, 1966–1990*, MIT Press, Cambridge MA, 1991, p. 18. The expression 'all art, after Duchamp' is deliberately ambiguous. It refers at once to both art produced after and in the wake of the reception of

Duchamp's works, and all art *tout court*, insofar as what an artwork is, is retrospectively determined by the subsequent history of works. That is, its reception is ontologically constitutive; its after-life is part of its life.

5 See Pierre Bourdieu, 'The Field of Cultural Production; or: The Economic World Reversed', in his *The Field of Cultural Production: Essays on Art and Literature*, Polity Press, Cambridge, 1993, Ch. 1.

6 See Danto, 'The End of Art'. This leads Danto into the contradictory waters of an 'art after the end of art' – not in Hegel's sense of a continuation of art after it has ceded its culturally formative role to the 'higher form' of philosophy – which is a continuation of art in its 'old', and for Hegel its only sense, but without its former power; but in the sense of a newly philosophical kind of art, the very idea of which belies the idea of art's end. See also Arthur Danto, *After the End of Art: Contemporary Art and the Pale of History*, Princeton University Press, Princeton, 1997. Oddly, it is not conceptual art which Danto has in mind in this discourse of the end of art, but Warhol. For Danto's personal distance from conceptual art as a movement in the New York artworld of the late 1960s and early 1970s, see his remarks in the interview 'Art and Analysis', *Radical Philosophy* 90 (July/August 1998), pp. 33–41.

7 I attempt such an elaboration in the survey essay which opens my *Conceptual Art*, Phaidon, London, forthcoming 2001.

8 Sol LeWitt, 'Paragraphs on Conceptual Art', in Charles Harrison and Paul Wood (eds), *Art in Theory*, Blackwell, Oxford, 1992, p. 834.

9 Henry Flynt, 'Concept Art', in La Monte Young (ed.), *An Anthology*, New York, 1963.

10 *Art in Theory*, p. 835.

11 Robert Morris, 'Anti-Form' (1968), in his *Continuous Project Altered Daily*, MIT Press, Cambridge, MA, 1993, pp. 41–3. Emphasis added.

12 *Art in Theory*, p. 835.

13 Flynt, 'Concept Art'.

14 *Art in Theory*, p. 836.

15 Sol LeWitt, 'Sentences on Conceptual Art', in *Art in Theory*, p. 839.

16 *Art in Theory*, pp. 834–6. Emphasis added.

17 Ibid., pp. 837–8.

18 Adrian Piper, interview with the author, March 1998, New York. I benefited greatly from this interview in conceiving the structure of this essay. Piper's writings have been collected as *Out of Order, Out of Sight. Volume 1: Selected Writings in Meta-Art 1968–1992* and *Volume 2: Selected Writings in Art Criticism, 1967–1992*, MIT Press, Cambridge, MA, 1996.

19 Kosuth, *Art After Philosophy and After*, p. 18.

20 The distinction between an abstract, and hence indeterminate, negation and a concrete or determinate negation – in which the determinacy of that which is negated is carried over into the product of the negation – derives from the two-stage account of negation in Hegel's dialectical logic. Such a logic is essentially retrospective in its establishment of determinate connections between historical forms. My claim that Kosuth effectively treats the idea of the propositional nature of art (art work as proposition about the nature of art) as a determinate or 'second' negation of the aesthetic conception of art is thus a retrospective, interpretative one, rather than a description of his self-understanding.

21 See Ad Reinhardt, 'Art as Art' (1962), in his *Art as Art: The Selected Writings of Ad Reinhardt*, University of California Press, Berkeley, 1975, pp. 53–6.

22 Pierre Cabanne, *Dialogues with Marcel Duchamp*, Da Capo, New York, n.d., p. 77.

23 Kosuth, *Art After Philosophy and After*, pp. 20, 26.
24 Ibid., p. 14.
25 Ibid., pp. 16, 20.
26 Ibid., pp. 19–20.
27 Charles Harrison, 'The Conditions of Problems', in his *Essays on Art & Language*, Blackwell, Oxford, 1991, pp. 93–4.
28 Kosuth, 'Art as Idea as Idea: An Interview with Jeanne Siegel', in *Art After Philosophy and After*, p. 53. Kosuth uses the multiplicity of Ad Reinhardt's practices as his example here, in conscious contradiction to Reinhardt's own idea of 'art as art'.
29 Seth Siegelaub, in Lucy Lippard, *Six Years: The Dematerialization of the Art Object 1966–1972*, University of California Press, Berkeley, 1973, p. 125.
30 Wall, *Dan Graham's Kammerspiel*, pp. 100, 102.
31 Adrian Piper describes Art & Language as 'creating a kind of private language'. Interview, March 1998.
32 Introduction, *Art-Language* vol.1, no.1 (May 1969), p. 10.
33 *Art-Language*, vol.1, no. 4. (November 1971), pp. 13, 27.
34 For a retrospective rationalization of these contortions as knowing strategic performances, see John Roberts, 'In Character', in Charles Harrison (ed.), *Art & Language in Practice, Vol. 2. Critical Symposium*, Fundació Antoni Tàpies, Barcelona, 1999, pp. 161–76.
35 See, for example, 'the astonishing but inescapable conclusion' of Michael Thompson's 'Conceptual Art: Category and Action' in the second issue of the journal: 'namely, that the seemingly erudite, scholastic, neutral, logical, austere, even incestuous, movement of conceptual art is, in fact, a naked bid for power at the very highest level – the wrestling from the groups at present at the top of our social structure, of control over the symbols of society', *Art-Language*, vol. 1, no. 2 (February 1970), p. 82.
36 See the remarks by Terry Atkinson explaining his decision to leave the group, in his *The Indexing, The World War One Moves and the Ruins of Conceptualism*, Circa Publications, Cornerhouse/Irish Museum of Modern Art, 1992.
37 Harrison, *Essays on Art & Language*, p. 75. Cf. also, p. 61.
38 Fredric Jameson, 'The Vanishing Mediator; or, Max Weber as Storyteller', in his *The Ideologies of Theory. Essays 1971–1986, Volume 2: The Syntax of History*, University of Minnesota Press, Minneapolis, 1988, p. 25.

7 DIALOGUE WITH PSYCHOANALYSIS

1 Jean Laplanche, *Essays on Otherness*, Routledge, London and New York, 1999.
2 Ibid., p. 257.
3 See in particular, 'The Unfinished Copernican Revolution' and 'Interpretation between Determinism and Hermeneutics: A Restatement of the Problem', in ibid., pp. 52–83 and 138–65; 'Psychoanalysis as Anti-Hermeneutics', *Radical Philosophy* 79 (Sept/Oct 1996), pp. 7–12; 'The Other Within: An Interview with Jean Laplanche', *Radical Philosophy* 102 (July/August 2000), pp. 31–41.
4 Laplanche's main work is the five-volume *Problématiques*, PUF, Paris, 1980–1987, in relation to which *New Foundations for Psychoanalysis* (1987), trans. David Macey, Blackwell, Oxford, 1989 represents a condensed summary of general results. For Laplanche's understanding of the concept of problematic, see the note by John Fletcher to the English edition of volume IV, Jean Laplanche, *The Unconscious and Id*, trans. Luke Thurston and Lindsay Watson, Rebus Press, London, 1999, pp. vii-ix.

5 *New Foundations*, Pt. 3. It is important to note that this 'theory of seduction' is a theory of the *interpellation* of the child by the adult's unconscious desire; it does not posit *actual* seduction, in the sense of child sexual abuse. The child is seduced by the enigma of the adult's desire, not by the adult as such. It does, however, offer a framework for the psychoanalytical interpretation of child sexual abuse, by drawing attention to those conditions of its possibility which characterize all adult–child relations.

6 For a reconstruction of these relations, see my *The Politics of Time*, pp. 104–12.

7 Despite the apparent oddity of the formulation, Laplanche is insistent that it is the message to which the demand adheres, not the adult him- or herself, since the desire that it conveys is unconscious, and there is no subject of the unconscious. See 'The Other Within', p. 41. For an account of demand-response as the structure of the ethical as such, in a variety of recent French thinkers, see Simon Critchley, 'Demanding Approval: On the Ethics of Alain Badiou', *Radical Philosophy* 100 (March/April 2000), pp. 16–27.

8 Cf. ch. 1, note 42, above.

9 Sigmund Freud, 'The Resistances to Psychoanalysis' (1925), in *Historical and Expository Works on Psychoanalysis*, trans. James Strachey, Penguin Freud Library, Vol. 15, Harmondsworth, 1986, p. 268.

10 Sigmund Freud, *Introductory Lectures on Psychoanalysis*, trans. James Strachey, Penguin Freud Library, Vol. 1, Harmondsworth, 1973, p. 496.

11 Michel Henry, *The Genealogy of Psychoanalysis* (1985), trans. Douglas Brick, Stanford University Press, Stanford, 1993, pp. 1–10; Jacques Lacan, *Ecrits: A Selection*, trans. Alan Sheridan, Tavistock, London, 1977, p. 1. Cf. Mikkel Borch-Jacobsen, *The Emotional Tie: Psychoanalysis, Mimesis, and Affect*, trans. Douglas Brick *et al.*, Stanford University Press, Stanford, 1993, pp. 123–4.

12 Sigmund Freud, *On Metapsychology*, Penguin Freud Library, Vol. 11, Harmondsworth, 1984, p. 351.

13 Cf. Slavoj Zizek, *The Ticklish Subject: The Absent Centre of Political Ontology*, Verso, London and New York, 1999.

14 I do not mean by this remark to question the essential continuity between the normal and the pathological that Freud intended these forays to establish. Rather, I am concerned with the relationship of psychoanalytical knowledge as a form of *self*-knowledge to knowledge of cultural objects and practices more generally.

15 'Time and the Other', *Essays on Otherness*, p. 256.

16 Ibid., p. 258.

17 Activity/passivity is the ontological binary most commonly associated with gendering in Western culture and the later Freud alike. For Laplanche, however, following Freud's earlier work, which stresses the gender indifference of childhood sexuality, such gendering is the result of 'secondary elaborations' subsequent to the primal situation, which are built, ideologically, upon the homology of the activity/passivity binary to that of adult/child. For an account of the contradictory and destructive effects of such a gendering, see Lynne Segal, *Straight Sex: The Politics of Pleasure*, Virago, London, 1994, ch. 4 and *Slow Motion: Changing Masculinities, Changing Men*, Virago, London, 1990, ch. 8.

18 The Lacanian Symbolic, Judith Butler has convincingly argued, reflects a heterosexist 'hegemonic imaginary', 'Gender and Performance: An Interview with Judith Butler', in Osborne (ed.), *A Critical Sense*, pp. 118–20.

19 J. Laplanche and J-B. Pontalis, 'Fantasy and the Origins of Sexuality' (1964), *International Journal of Psycho-Analysis* 49 (1968). See, for example, Leo

Bersani's recent use of this model in his proliferation of the Oedipal triangle into a 'fantasmatic orgy' with ten figures, in his 'Against Monogamy', *The Oxford Literary Review* 20, *Beyond Redemption: The Work of Leo Bersani*, pp. 3–22. However, symptomatically, Bersani discusses monogamy only at the level of psychic identification, as a fixity of desire. Oddly, for someone writing about fantasy, he appears to presuppose a one-to-one correspondence between desire and practice. He thus never approaches the more pertinent issue: the complex relationship between structures of desire and practices.

20 'The Other Within', p. 37.

21 Frederic Jameson, *Postmodernism, or, the Cultural Logic of Late Capitalism*, Verso, London, 1991, ch. 1; Slavoj Zizek, *The Plague of Fantasies*, Verso, London and New York, 1998. Zizek himself maintains that his analysis constitutes a form of the critique of political economy, in opposition to more fashionable culturalist tendencies, since 'the thrust of Capital' is 'the Real of our time'. Unfortunately, however, this identification would appear to be secured on the basis of a parallel use of capital letters alone, rather than anything which might count as an analysis. Zizek, *The Ticklish Subject*, p. 4. For a critique of the general tendency in recent philosophy to substantivize adjectives, thereby creating bogus abstract entities with an efficacy of their own (the Symbolic, the Maternal, the Originary, the Negative ...), see Laplanche, 'A Short Treatise on the Unconscious', in *Essays on Otherness*, pp. 114–16. Psychoanalysis does, however, make a claim for the metaphysical realism of the unconscious. On Laplanche's view, 'it may be the only remaining metaphysical cause'. 'The Other Within', p. 36.

22 *New Foundations for Psychoanalysis*, p. 84.

23 There was a period during which Freud conceived of treatment as a process in which the analyst might discover the relevant unconscious material and communicate it to the patient. However, by 1917 it was already clear to him that: '*Our* knowledge about the unconscious material is not equivalent to *his* knowledge; if we communicate our knowledge to him, he does not receive it *instead of* his unconscious material, but *beside* it; and that makes very little change in it', *Introductory Lectures*, p. 488.

24 Ibid., pp. 496–8.

25 Ibid., p. 498. For a conceptual genealogy of the term in Freud's works and the main developments of the concept by subsequent analysts, see the entry in Jean Laplanche and J-B. Pontalis, *The Language of Psychoanalysis*, trans. Donald Nicholson-Smith, Karnac Books, London, 1988, pp. 455–62.

26 'Psychoanalysis as Anti-Hermeneutics', p. 11.

27 Laplanche, 'The Drive and its Source Objects: Its Fate in the Transference', *Essays on Otherness*, p. 131.

28 *New Foundations for Psychoanalysis*, p. 164.

29 'Transference: Its Provocation by the Analyst', *Essays on Otherness*, p. 222.

30 Ibid., pp. 224, 226, 233.

31 *New Foundations for Psychoanalysis*, pp. 160–2.

32 Cf. Adorno's account of the enigma of the work of art, in *Aesthetic Theory*, trans. Robert Hullot-Kentor, Minnesota University Press, Minneapolis, 1997, pp. 119–25. Laplanche may be considered to offer a communicational psychoanalytical grounding for Adorno's modernist ontology of the art work. It is important to note that it is autonomous art *per se* which is constitutively enigmatic, on this account, not some particular type or body of work. This is a reprise of Friedrich Schlegel's Romantic motif of 'incomprehensibility' to which psychoanalysis is itself undoubtedly indebted. See Friedrich Schlegel 'On

Incomprehensibility', in Jochen Schulte-Sasse *et al.* (eds.), *Theory as Practice: A Critical Anthology of Early German Romantic Writings*, University of Minnesota Press, Minneapolis, 1997, pp. 118–27.

33 Sigmund Freud, 'Constructions in Analysis' (1937), *The Standard Edition of the Complete Psychological Works of Sigmund Freud*, edited and translated by James Strachey, Hogarth Press, London, 1953–1974, Vol. XXIII, pp. 265–6.

34 'A Short Treatise on the Unconscious', *Essays on Otherness*, p. 112.

35 'Psychoanalysis as Anti-Hermeneutics', pp. 12, 9.

36 Jacques Derrida, 'Resistances', in *Resistances of Psychoanalysis* (1996), trans. Peggy Kamuf *et al.*, Stanford University Press, Stanford, 1998, pp. 19–20.

37 Ibid., p. 20.

INDEX